THINKING IN COLOR
CAN CHANGE YOUR LIFE!

"By thinking along with me, you will become a different person. You will understand people better. And as a result, you will become more effective and successful in your personal, professional and business relations. You will feel freer inside, and less dependent on the outer world. By changing yourself, you will also be changing your surroundings. The inner freedom that you achieve, the ability to make demands, as well as to do without, will make you independent. Hence, you will very likely form new relationships and even break off those you still put up with today."

REALIZE YOUR TRUE POTENTIAL
<u>AS THE 4-COLOR PERSON!</u>

D1010053

Also by Dr. Max Lüscher

The Lüscher Color Test

Published by POCKET BOOKS

The
4-Color Person
Dr. Max Lüscher

TRANSLATED FROM THE GERMAN BY

Joachim Neugroschel

PUBLISHED BY POCKET BOOKS NEW YORK

POCKET BOOKS, a Simon & Schuster division of
GULF & WESTERN CORPORATION
1230 Avenue of the Americas, New York, N.Y. 10020

Contents

1

THE 4-COLOR PERSON

GREEN: SELF-RESPECT

YELLOW: SELF-DEVELOPMENT

RED: SELF-CONFIDENCE

BLUE: SELF-MODERATION

SELF-EVALUATION

2

THE NON-4-COLOR PERSON

3

THE COLORS

4

THE PSYCHOLOGY AND PHILOSOPHY OF THE 4-COLOR PERSON

1

THE
4-COLOR
PERSON

Elements of Self-Realization

You've just bought this book. What do you expect to get out of it? Pleasant entertainment, worthwhile instruction? Or have you and your bookcase had more than enough of all that?

Do you realize that reading, just like TV, is never anything but a vicarious experience? In both, things happen only "as though" they were real life. The scenes, plots, and thoughts go on "as if" you were there. But something like a thick glass wall always separates you from the action. You're of no importance. The pretty girl in the commercial smiles in the same seductive way whether you're devotedly genuflecting in front of the tube or going to the bathroom. In addition to being vicarious, a book doesn't permit any true dialogue either. And to many people, I grant you, books are nothing more than wall decorations. But when you take a book to bed in order to read yourself to sleep, you become a world traveler, a private eye, or even a revolutionary, until you lay the book aside and doze off, or make love to tire yourself out.

As author and reader, we cannot personally question and answer each other. Just as with television, no true dialogue or discussion is possible. This makes it very hard to reach my goals for you and me: self-understanding and self-realization. The impossibility of true dialogue is the curse of all books. Great things may take place within them, but only "as if" and "as though," and not as experienced reality. I would like to jump out of this book and ask you why you're reading *The 4-Color Person* instead of just being affectionate to your spouse or lover. I would like you to know it doesn't bother me in the least if you yawn your head off while reading this book. But you're a poor conversationalist if you let me do all the talking—that is, if you don't even bother to think, make decisions, or begin acting.

Let me come to the point. You want to find out who this 4-Color Person is.

As you already know, a harmonious color disk can be constructed from the four basic colors: yellow, red, blue, and green. The circle is the symbol of totality and harmony. As you also know (or at least suspect), each color arouses a definite feeling within you. Red, for instance, gives you a completely different sensation than dark blue. Red affects all people in the same way, no matter how old they are or what culture they live in. It's always exciting, stimulating, activating. It expresses vital force and self-confidence. Dark blue, on the other hand, always conveys rest and relaxation. It corresponds to a state of satisfaction, contentment, security (the blue mantle of the Virgin Mary), and serenity. Fir-green, if it's bluish and dark, strikes everyone as hard and solid. It matches a feeling of inner stability, persistence, consistency, self-assertion, and self-confidence. The person who feels solid and secure has a firmly rooted sense of self-esteem. Bright yellow always triggers a gay, light, free, open feeling. It has a liberating, loosening effect. Therefore it corresponds to a definite sense of freedom and self-development.

Thus, a 4-Color Person experiences, thinks, and acts out of four "senses of self." These are:

- Stable self-respect (green)
- Active self-confidence (red)
- Contented self-moderation (blue)
- Open-minded self-development (yellow)

Four-Color People are harmoniously realized in all four areas—that is to say, in their totality. They are happy people who experience more intensely than most people, and who always find life fascinating.

Don't worry. I'm not trying to palm a new morality off on you. Moralizing and superstition are alien to the 4-Color Person. We experience each moment, open ourselves up to the things of the world, understand their connections, and then classify them. When we see something of the world, we're happy.

I'm no pedantic recluse. My friends, my beloved, life's delicacies, a rippling lake, an exhilarating ski slope—these are all more important to me than the illusions centering around prestige and prominence, those two follies.

A life that is truly lived comes about through interaction: in society, in dialogues, in the give-and-take between mother and child, employer and employee, even between a person and his or her tasks, creator and his or her work. The 4-Color Person wants to get all the knowledge, joy, and pleasure out of life that is possible. Happiness is the goal of 4-Color People. That's what gives meaning to their lives, which can only be lived once. In order to be happy, they develop their minds. For by doing so, they sharpen their sensory perceptions, draw pleasure from a thousand sources, and come to understand themselves and their friends and opponents.

Conventional prejudices and superstitions, sown in us by government, religion, and science, find no fertile soil in 4-Color People. Like bloodhounds, they sniff out all the motives and reasons behind these things. They relentlessly ask "Why?" about everything concerning themselves and the world around them. They don't stop questioning until they have dealt with all the problems gnawing at them. It is only after freeing themselves, as far as possible, from problems, from inner and outer compulsions, that they can feel good.

Although you still really know very little about the 4-Color Person, this first meeting has already made you like and trust, or be indifferent to, or even dislike, him or her. But, if that person is not your cup of tea, then close the book, and send it, in its impaired chastity, to someone you don't care for.

On the other hand, if you would like to know the 4-Color Person better, and thereby get tremendous insight, intense experience, and great joy and pleasure out of life, you must first realize one thing: Not only are you going to spend many hours with this book, in a very personal dialogue with me, but you are also embarking on the adventure of change.

By thinking along with me, you will become a different person. You will understand people better. And as a result, you will become more effective and successful in your personal, professional, and business relations. You will feel freer inside, and less dependent on the outer world. By changing yourself, you will also be changing your surroundings. The inner freedom that you achieve, the ability to make demands, as well as to do without, will make you independent. Hence, you will very likely form new relationships, and even break off those you still put up with today.

If you have decided to keep reading, then we will have an intellectual friendship. It will be an intimate relationship, for I am not stating just any opinion that you can interpret for yourself, or even skip, whichever you like—I'm going to tell you what I think of you personally! If, for instance, I define the Spineless Puppet and, by chance, everything I say about that person happens to fit you, then it should be understood, between friends, that I would include you in that category. Naturally I hope our dialogue doesn't make you feel worse than helpless in any situation. I hope you'll feel like the Lucky Devil, who was born with a silver spoon in his mouth, and who can roar with laughter.

Good, you're still with me. I want us to be close. We will be dealing with many things requiring sincere and mutual trust. Besides, I like you—because you're still with me, and you don't seem to be a self-complacent, hypersensitive mimosa or a crashing bore, a conceited know-it-all, or a puppet who worships authority. But after all, you bought this book not to become buddy-buddy with me but to get to the heart of the 4-Color Person. So, I'll get to the point.

You are probably wondering why I call this individual the Color Person. Elbow Person, Stomach Person, or Money Person sounds a bit more concrete. You'd certainly like to know why this is the "4-Color Person" and not the "2-Color Person" or even the "17-Color Person."

4-ness

There are four colors for much the same reason as there are four directions on the compass and four seasons in the year. The 4-ness is rooted in our thinking. There are four categories of thought that we apply to something we are trying to understand. When we want to judge something, we divide what originally appears as a unit. We separate it into two opposites: for example, humanity, into men and women.

Thus, a judgment comes by dividing into two antitheses.

Every judgment becomes more apt if we follow the first division into opposites with a second division. Two times two is four.

That's how we get four elements or four categories of thought or four types. Here are a few examples. For clarity, I'll add the corresponding color:

The four elements:

fire	red
water	blue
air	yellow
earth	green

The four temperaments:

choleric	red
phlegmatic	blue
sanguine	yellow
melancholy	green

That's how we have to consider the four types in C. G. Jung, Erich Fromm, Karen Horney, V. E. Frankl, F. Riemann, and many others. Even Freud has the very same categories with:

genital	red
oral	blue
anal	green

And naturally, he would have hit upon the 4-ness if he hadn't made the Freudian slip of forgetting that important erotic area, visual sex, which corresponds to yellow. Now since the 4-ness is intrinsic to human thinking, I too will speak about four colors. You'll find more about the reasons for the 4-ness and about the psychology of the four colors in Part Three of this book. Anything we need at this point to understand The 4-Color Person will be summed up in key words in the following table.

I'll match up the four colors with their sensations and behavior. But most important for me are the four senses of self to which these four colors unconsciously appeal. It's crucial for you to feel what the color expresses, to see that the pertinent sense of self corresponds to this same mood. Thus red, for instance, as activity, corresponds to the sense of self for strength and self-confidence, while dark blue, as relaxation and satisfaction, matches a feeling of self-moderation. The

four senses of self are the four keys for opening up
your heaven on earth. They are the four cardinal
points of your inner world. They are the four normal
senses of self, and you have to hold the reins on them
tight, for the sake of your inner equilibrium—at any
price and in any situation. In that way, you'll stay in
the driver's seat and realize your full potential. That's
my fondest wish for you and for me. The 4-Color
Person's art of living consists in a virtuoso application
of these four faculties, these four senses of self.

COLOR	SENSATION	BEHAVIOR	SENSE OF SELF
Red	causes *excitement*	and *activity*	so: *self-confidence* (feeling of strength)
Blue	causes *tranquility*	and *satisfaction*	so: *self-moderation* (adjustment)
Green	causes *solidity*	and *persistence*	so: *self-respect* (identity)
Yellow	causes *expansion*	and *change*	so: *self-development* (freedom)

The four senses of self probably sound abstract at
this point, or even unintelligible. But I'll now explain
how you should think of them.

The Four Senses of Self

GREEN: SELF-RESPECT

You may feel that you're a very splendid bird, a peacock among artists, a peacock among managers, politicians, or scientists, among handsome men or beautiful women, or the biggest sheep in the sheep set, or the master of some guild.

This feeling of your own worth is known as arrogant pride. From now on, we'll call any exaggerated sense of self-worth *self-overrating*.

What do you think is the opposite of self-overrating? Don't just say an inferiority complex. There are several kinds.

If a person looks bashfully down like a trembling student when smelling the perfume of pleasure or success, then that individual is suffering from *self-doubt*.

Four-Color People are reasonable. They don't overestimate themselves. Nor do they suffer from self-doubt.

Aren't these just pious wishes I put in my Christmas stocking? You're right. Merely understanding connections won't change my sense of self. But then I didn't

assume you came into the world as a ready-made
4-Color Person.

The normal sense of self-worth, self-respect, is the
end product of your efforts at being genuine and
truthful with yourself. If you behave as demanded by
your conviction about yourself, then you'll feel that
you're genuine and true, that you're really yourself.
You'll feel your *identity*, as it's called today.

Four-Color People are eager to stay faithful to their
conviction and to behave according to the best of their
knowledge and conscience. "Act fair and don't be
afraid of anyone." That motto expresses the sovereign
self-respect of 4-Color People. They are noblemen.
They feel like the masters of their inner worlds. Their
steady effort to seek truth and act by it—to have the
courage of their conviction—gives 4-Color People a
feeling of authenticity, a feeling of worth, an *identity*.

Noblesse oblige. Nobility obligates. The very same
thing is meant by Immanuel Kant's renowned
"categorical imperative." As a philosopher, he was
able to formulate this guiding principle in such a way
that it can be an ethical axiom for all occasions: Act
according to principles which can at any time be valid
for a universal legislation.

The person who lives by such ground rules, the
person who lets such a conviction be his or her guide,
the person who decides and behaves in those
terms—that person has true nobility. The person who
feels committed to authenticity, who fulfills his or her
identity and satisfies his or her self-respect—that person will be referred to from now on as a *nobleman*.

YELLOW: SELF-DEVELOPMENT

A different sense of self is incorporated by the
Lucky Stiff, by Hans-in-Luck. Do you remember the
fairy tale? Hans got a lump of gold from his master as a

reward for his loyal services. But as he wandered along, the gold became so heavy that he traded it for a horse—and was very happy and felt very lucky. But the horse threw him off, so he traded it for a cow—and was very happy and felt very lucky. But the cow kicked him while he was milking her, and so he traded her for a pig—and felt happy and lucky. He swapped the pig for a goose, the goose for a heavy whetstone, which, luckily, he dropped into the well when he was about to have a drink. Light-hearted and free of any burden, he arrived home, happy and lucky. Hans-in-Luck, the Lucky Stiff, is the symbol for people who feel free and independent, who can give up anything they own and always choose the possibility that strikes them as the best and hence makes them feel happy and lucky.

Hans' increasing loss of external, material values shows that a person can feel free and independent only if he or she doesn't cling to worldly goods. For Lucky Stiffs, what counts is personal and not material worth. Of all possibilities, they choose only the one that is best for their situation, thereby giving them the most pleasure.

The self-development of the 4-Color Person is realized only in independence, in the ability to perceive the given possibilities, to make contacts, deepen relationships, experience all beautiful things, convert money value into experience value.

Here too, normal independence and self-development contrast with both abnormal overexaggeration and underexaggeration. Overexaggeration makes independence a self-delusion, an escape from oneself, a lack of responsibility ("That doesn't concern me"). Such people offer pseudo-objective arguments to evade responsibility. Their favorite sport is buck-passing.

The overresponsible are likewise abnormal. They suffer from compulsive perfectionism They burden themselves with imaginary guilt feelings, with self-accusations. They became cramped in their self-constraint. They think and say, "I absolutely have to. . . ."

RED: SELF-CONFIDENCE

You know about Robinson Crusoe, who was ship-wrecked on an island and forced to be totally self-reliant, thereby shaping a new life for himself. If you, as a child or as a parent with children, go camping with a tent and a pot—even if you just broil meat over a campfire—you feel like a little Robinson Crusoe.

There are Robinson Crusoes not only on desert islands, but also in industrial concerns, in disaster aid, in daring research and development projects. Any person with the courage to hazard something unknown is a Robinson Crusoe. People who try to master a new task on their own initiative, the man who changes a tire on his car for the first time, the woman who personally organizes a trip abroad for the first time, the man who has an idea and devotes all his energy and ability to making it come true—all these people have the pioneer blood of a Robinson Crusoe flowing in their veins. Through every great or small deed in which you are a big or little Robinson Crusoe, your self-confidence grows and consolidates.

Self-confidence is a further, a third, sense of self for 4-Color People. They have confidence in their abilities and in their physical and mental performance. Why? Not because they imagine some nonexistent power, but because their activities and achievements teach them what their real abilities are.

Four-Color People don't rest upon their laurels.

They don't see them as downy feathers. Feeling their own strength and abilities, they experience themselves only in an accomplishment so demanding that they don't feel overstrained, but above all not understrained. By being ready for achievement and challenge, the 4-Color Person gains self-confidence, which is necessary for realizing his or her full potential.

The man who is full of his own importance, like the "brave little tailor," who killed seven flies with one blow, lacks a normal self-confidence. As a boaster and braggart, he constantly overrates himself. By acting pompous and trying to impress others ("Will they ever be surprised!"), he is merely showing his *self-exaggeration*.

And vice versa: A lack of self-confidence results from being too undemanding of oneself. Women who limit themselves to reading magazines, working crossword puzzles, pursuing the science of dustrags; men who won't broaden their horizon with anything but the names of sports idols—all these people are weakening their self-confidence. They feel sorry for themselves; they squander their energy on *self-pity*.

BLUE: SELF-MODERATION

In the year 323 B.C. a man whom you know died in Corinth. His worldwide renown came not from wealth, nor power, nor any invention. His ideal was the opposite of any kind of prestige. What he aspired to was mental and material independence. Diogenes of Sinope was clever, coarsely funny, quick-witted, and strong-willed. He would have been capable of becoming a successful merchant or politician. But supposedly, he lived in a barrel. And when he saw another man drinking from his cupped hand, he supposedly even threw away his beaker. When Alexander the Great asked Diogenes if he had any wish that the monarch could grant, Diogenes asked him to step aside, he was blocking the sun.

We know of Diogenes as a philosopher of life in the school of Cynics. However much or little truth there may be to the anecdotes, one thing is certain: Self-moderation and contentment were the wise ideas that he taught and that made him immortal.

Self-moderation is the fourth sense of self, which the 4-Color Person needs as much as the other three. Four-Color People never put their heads in a yoke; they always adjust to the given possibilities. They not only have the self-confidence to make demands, they also have the strength and necessary feeling of self-worth to be able to do without or to give. When their perception of circumstances makes them realize that help is of the essence, then the unsaintly 4-Color People, like St. Martin, will share their cloaks with the needy. Their self-moderation makes them peace-loving and charitable.

The abnormality of exaggerated modesty, self-denial, *self-renunciation,* any kind of self-sacrifice (for true help is not felt to be sacrificial)—such inauthentic self-moderation is repugnant to 4-Color People. They can see through it, they know it to be hypocritical, dishonest, a form of blackmail ("I can't live without you").

The same holds true for *self-dissatisfaction,* the constant fear of getting the dirty end of the stick, continual and endless greed for more and more. These things are alien to the 4-Color Person, who lives in fullness, not emptiness, in the present, not the future.

SELF-EVALUATION

The normality and self-realization of the 4-Color Person consist in his or her knack of maintaining an inner balance with these four senses of self.

SENSE OF SELF	SYMBOLIC COLOR
Self-respect ("nobleman") (authenticity, fidelity to conviction, "identity," behavior in line with conviction)	Green
Self-development ("Hans-in-Luck") (taking advantage of the given possibilities; independence, freedom)	Yellow
Self-confidence ("Robinson Crusoe") (readiness for achievement; use of personal strength and faculties)	Red
Self-moderation ("Diogenes") (adjustment to the given possibilities; readiness to do without or to give)	Blue

As we have seen in the earlier discussion, each of the four normal senses of self is matched by an abnormal overevaluation of oneself and an abnormal underevaluation of oneself.

I would like to collect these three stages of the senses of self in a table. And I would like to ask you to think about which of your friends could be most aptly put in these twelve categories. Whom do you know who overrates himself in arrogant pride? Or whom do you know who suffers from secret self-doubts and hence appears blasé? Go through all your fellow beings and try to find the right person for some of the twelve senses of self!

And where do *you* fit in? Did you find yourself in the

box for self-overevaluation or self-underevaluation?
Or among the four normal senses of self?

Which of the four normal senses of self are well
developed in you? In which do you slip into over- or
underevaluation of yourself?

COLOR	NORMAL SENSE OF SELF (=)	SELF-OVEREVALUATION (+)	SELF-UNDEREVALUATION (−)
Green	self-respect (nobleman)	self-overrating	self-doubt
Yellow	self-development (Hans-in-Luck)	self-escape	self-compulsion
Red	self-confidence (Robinson Crusoe)	overconfidence	self-pity
Blue	self-moderation (Diogenes)	self-renunciation	self-dissatisfaction

Do you notice how quickly and easily you feel that
another person is a self-important braggart or a kind-
hearted angel?

You needn't fool yourself any longer. Other people
can tell whether you overrate yourself, undervalue
yourself, or are modest.

Your words, your voice, your eyes, your body language, your clothes, and a hundred other signals are
unconsciously picked up by everyone else. All these
expressions are registered by every adult, every child,
every dog, and intuitively ordered into a judgment. All
the "personality signals" betray not only who you'd
like to be, but also how you really feel. They reveal
your sense of self.

Try the following. Switch off the sound on your TV
and just watch, or else observe people whom you don't
know. Read their facial expressions and body language

and try to tell which of the four senses of self are lodged in those people. In this way, you'll learn how to listen to your feelings. You'll learn how to form a clearer and more conscious opinion of other people.

Perhaps there is really no faculty more useful or more important than this one: to properly recognize and understand other human beings.

Well, are you a 4-Color Person? Of course, you've got the stuff for it, as long as you can muster the courage for ruthless honesty with yourself.

You may ask, "Is Lüscher himself totally honest? Is *he* capable of the things he expects of me? Who can possibly be unconditionally honest with himself?"

Do what I do. Make every effort to be honest and don't give up. Honesty and all the other qualities we've been speaking about aren't trophies that you can win and carry around in your moral collection forever.

Your honesty and mine depend on the extent to which we can maintain our inner balance even in difficult situations. That's the way it is with any quality. All our qualities and faculties are effective only when, and as long as, we use them. So do it. As they say, "Today is the first day of the rest of your life."

The Human Specialty: Inner Balance

Even if you haven't asked in so many words, you always keep wondering "Who am I really?" You know that outside of yourself, a lot of living creatures run, swim, and fly on the earth. You regard yourself as something special. You're proud to be a human being and not just some creature or other. Now what is the special feature of mankind?

The biologists see something unique in man's upright walk. Granted, that saves us a second pair of shoes. But does that make a human being anything special? Man is the only living creature to possess language. At least, that's what the biologists claim, although they know not only that birds twitter mating calls or warnings to each other, but even that whales deep in the ocean can carry on dialogues. Man has specially developed hands and a specially developed brain, others argue. A dog would calmly retort: "And I have a specially developed nose."

You know that the giraffe has a particularly long neck. You know that the falcon has a particularly keen eye. You know that the gazelle has a particularly fast leap. And you know from religious instruction that man is particularly special.

Since religions teach faith and not knowledge, you know that man is particularly special for a very specific reason. You've heard that some of these particularly special creatures end up in hell, but that the particularly good special creatures will be jubilant in heaven for all eternity.

So, along with all his bodily disadvantages, what is so special about man as opposed to the other mammals?

Natural science has a hard time defining the crucial specialty of man in contrast to animals. On the other hand, the Christian religion solves the problem with bold elegance. What makes man so special among all living creatures is that he is the only animate being to enter heaven or hell in the afterlife.

And that indeed is the very trait that distinguishes humans from all other beings. Man lives either in hell or in heaven, though not in the afterlife. It is the daily hell of his conflict-ridden self-estimation in which man lives—unless, as a 4-Color Person, he or she uses daily self-realization to achieve inner balance and live in a heaven on earth. You, in your real life, can choose between heaven and hell. And that's what makes man so special.

Animals probably experience their environment more alertly and subtly than man. In contrast, man judges and evaluates his ego, his position in regard to other people, far more alertly and subtly than any animal.

Untiring positive or negative self-estimations, life moods as created by a sense of self, are what make man so special. They are what constitute a personal heaven or hell. Animals do not seem to have these self-estimations and senses of self, which derive from an inner constitution. That's why animals never get into the heaven or hell of a sense of self. These are inevitable only for people, because they have to live with them.

We 4-Color People leave the heaven above the earth to the angels and sparrows. But in our earthly paradise, we want to spread out and celebrate our festivals.

As a 4-Color Person, you know the four cardinal points which you have to reach in order to realize your potential. You strive to act by the royal motto *Noblesse oblige*. You follow new paths as Robinson Crusoe, renounce smilingly as Diogenes, and maintain your independence as Hans-in-Luck. But you really feel you're in heaven when these four masters not only enjoy utmost health and mental freshness, but also get along with one another and achieve a harmonious equilibrium.

Thus, the special feature of 4-Color People is that they feel they're in the heaven of their self-realization once they've found their inner balance among the four senses of self.

Most people know where to find their toothbrush, their wallet, their bottle of whiskey, and their sexual satisfaction. But where can they find their inner balance? Many people don't even ask themselves that question.

Without your inner balance, you can only be a 1- or 2-Color Person, and you'll have no chance of being truly happy. So you ask, "Where do I find my inner balance?"

There are two widespread excuses for lacking this balance, for living in hell. Some people think that man is a product of his genes. Others think he's the product of his upbringing and environment, the social and economic conditions he lives in. Sometimes heredity and sometimes society are regarded as crucial for a person's essence. Both factors certainly play a part. But the decisive factor is something else.

I am very interested in clearly showing you what this third thing is. Statistical investigations with color tests have shown me that in our society at least 65% of all adults could fundamentally improve their lives if they only recognized the prime importance of this third factor.

At the same time, I know that, strictly speaking, I can't teach you anything that hasn't come to you long since from experience. I can only induce you to become fully conscious of your experience and to put it in the right perspective.

Since a picture, or an image, is worth a thousand words, I want to clarify my point with a symbol. Do you remember when you were learning how to ride a bike?

First, you had to have a bike. Let's compare this technological vehicle to the body and the genotype. Now among bicycles, there are racers and bulkier models. There are attractive and elegant, twisted and rusty bikes. Some have technical defects, which correspond to bad or sick genes. We can compare the street conditions to the social and economic situation in which you have to live. There are smooth roads and bumpy roads. Some offer constant surprises with potholes. Some are arduously steep. Others descend so rapidly that you can burn out your brakes or crack your head.

But most important of all is you yourself, the cyclist. You've been shown that you have to step on the pedal to make the bicycle move. Let's compare that to your daily activity. The person who doesn't pedal, who isn't active, will fall on his or her face. The person who zooms off headlong will risk having a skid and crashing to the ground.

You've also been shown how to steer left, right, or straight ahead. Let's compare the steering with your aiming deliberately at a specific goal.

Any teacher can easily show you any of these things so that you can imitate them. But you know that the best bicycle (genotype), the best street conditions (social circumstances), and the pedaling (activity) and steering (goals) won't make you move an inch if you don't fulfill one premise that no master can inculcate in you: No one can teach you how to keep your balance. That's one thing you have to discover in yourself and by yourself. The instructor can certainly run alongside you and hold you in balance on the seat. But that's really the only assistance he can offer. And then comes the moment when the experience overcomes you: "I've got it! I can do it!"

Suddenly you feel you're balanced and you know how to stay balanced. Now you try to maintain this feeling or rediscover it in case you lose your balance.

My dear 4-Color Person, do you understand what I'm trying to tell you with this experience of balance? As an infant, you had to find your balance when you were learning how to walk. And you have to find your balance anew every time you learn a new physical skill—skiing, ballet, wielding a violin bow.

The same holds true for the mind and the soul. You have to strive for inner balance in the hour of supreme happiness and at the hour of your death. It is this third factor, inner balance, that makes up the intrinsic special feature of human beings. It is the human quality *par excellence*.

If you're firm in your seat and if you can find your

equilibrium at any time, in any situation, then you've got the makings of a full-blooded 4-Color Person.

As we all know, God finished his six-day opus with man. So we're Saturday's and not Sunday's children. One man feels it in his back. Another has to run around on flat feet all his life. Our bodies are, as we know, not always the best vehicles. Whether you have the strength and health of a Hercules and the beauty of an Adonis or a bulldog—it's all a matter of luck, good or bad. You have to resign yourself. The bike is yours. Your body is made available to you as ramshackle as it is. You know very well that your body is merely that part of your environment that is closest to you. Only women and men whose good looks exceed their intelligence sometime believe that they themselves are the attractive vehicle. For us, however, the body remains a part of the outer world—the part giving us the most sensory pleasure and pain. But it's not just a matter of the vehicle. The street conditions, i.e., the circumstances of milieu, also form our outer world. Depending on whether the stork dropped you in a cradle with a sack of straw or a sack of money, at least the first third of your life runs clearly in one style or another. You were put in the boat as a boy or a girl, as an only child or one of several children. And that will decide whether you become a deckhand or a captain in life, whether you'll have clear sailing or stormy weather.

If you have to sacrifice the best years of your life in a senseless war, if intolerance get the upper hand among the anarchists or facists, among leftists or rightists, among Christians or anti-Christians, then you can be glad if you still find you way.

My dear 4-Color Person, you've laughed a couple of times. But you know how serious the bicycle allegory is. And I have to confess, I was really afraid I might not make it clear enough for you. For if the thing about balance hadn't become a powerful experience for you, if you hadn't told yourself "Of course, I have to stay in the seat no matter what, even if it rains cats and dogs," then I'd have the same feeling I had in school when the teacher said, "Lüscher, I'm sorry, but I can only give you an F again."

As things have turned out, I do have a good feeling. And I'm looking forward to tackling the next stronghold: normality.

This and the overall plenitude depend. The outer world can begin to use its attractions again to pull him through, stop, and keep it. You'll have a steadier, better, far more solid and secure hold. You'll stay upright, straight, and clearly distribute the weight of your body around your I-point.

The Normal Person

Everybody probably has to deal with two realities at all times: his or her outer and inner worlds. At the very center of this inner world, a certain being, the very one that says *I* to itself, is trying to maintain its balance and stay in its seat.

You don't have to look very far. All around you, there are *I*'s that keep falling off their seats, that plunge into holes, and that have to catapult themselves aloft as though they were bouncing up and down on a trampoline. But then they regularly plummet down again and, with a new start, they jump up over themselves. Next to the trampoline people, who leap into the air themselves, there are others. These others are like a Ping-Pong ball. They allow their boss, spouse, beloved, or archenemy to hurl them across the net and from corner to corner.

But you as a future 4-Color Person aren't just an *I*-sayer: "I would think" or "I would prefer." You *are* and you *feel* yourself to be: *I. I* on the seat and in balance. You're active and you've got a firm grip on the handlebars. From your solid *I*-point, you unfold your activity, on all sides, all around. The circle around your *I*-point is bigger or smaller according to your strength, your abilities, your energy. And the better, the more sensibly, the more carefully, the more well-balanced the way you steer your strength, abilities, and energy, then the rounder the arc of your circle around your *I*-point.

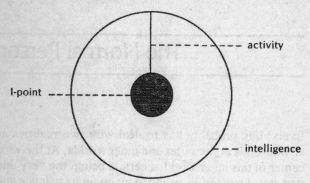

That's how our *innter world* functions. As we know, it is constantly surrounded by a second reality, the outside world. That's why I draw the outside world as an outer circle around the first circle.

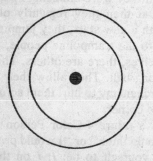

The earth's rotation isn't completely circular. Our planet always wobbles. Somewhere in the outer world, the devil is always on the loose. A fine, evenly round external world, a "healthy world," has never existed. Only your own inner world can be a "healthy world" insofar as you keep your *I* balanced.

In the outer world, there are constant protuberances, collisions, and depressions. Here, the outer world has had bumps and pits.

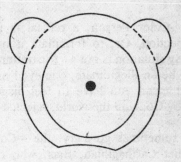

And here, there's been a collision.

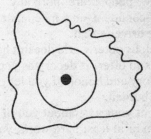

But in the 4-Color Person, the ego has maintained its balance and his or her inner world is as round as can be. Translated into everyday English, this means the following:

Even when you've been refused something, you're

far from disappointed. Because you've got your inner balance, you would never dream of letting a bump in the outer world, a failure, cause a depression in your inner world. Strictly speaking, no one else can ever get in there. Here you make the bumps and pits yourself. Do you feel sorry for yourself? Have you observed how children love to cry with epicurean relish? How they use some trivial reason to gloat inwardly over an outer bump?

For the 4-Color Person, a refusal is far from a personal rejection. Or, to formulate it on a higher level: A lousy situation is not a "frustration."

You may be an illegitimate, one-eyed orphan. But that doesn't mean you have to feel disadvantaged, abandoned by God and the world, rejected and "frustrated."

If things sometimes go awry, the 4-Color Person feels like that Carthaginian, Bias, who commented upon the loss of his entire wealth with the famous words *Omnia mea mecum porto* ("I have everything that's mine on me").

That's how people are normally: sovereign and modest, self-confident and independent. And hence always in the driver's seat.

The capricious outer world doesn't have just failures and accidents to offer. It decorates you and loads you down with glory and honors if you let yourself be used as a beast of burden.

If you've got your wits about you, if you're capable of enthusiasm or at least hard work, you cannot avoid success. It's like an ulcer. It festers. The circle of your outer world does not remain round. The bumps of your success reveal your proficiency. You become a "born" businessman, career person, expert, lady's man, social lion, a much-courted girl or a fulltime mother, a housewife or someone who wears her heart on her sleeve. Are you successful? Do you become the lackey and victim of your successes? Are you mirrored in them? Do you polish your image like your shoes— until it glows? Is the jet set your bellwether? Or do you trot after some other sheep set? If so, then you make yourself dependent on this role in society. You are a thrall to your craving for prestige, even if you become president of all presidents and the brightest star of all the starlings.

Whatever the outer world may be like, whether the outer circle bulges in or out, the inner circle—the 4-Color Person's *I*—remains balanced, keeps its utterly round harmony. The inner world is immune to all tribulations (pits) and temptations (bumps).

Do you think I'm trying to give you a shot of hypocritical morality? I have to ask you more precisely: Do you have the impression I'm trying to influence you, so that you'll turn into some silly ideal?

Not on your life. You're not supposed to turn into *anyone else's* ideal. You're just to become what you really are: yourself. That's what I want, and that's probably what you want too. What I'm after is nothing less than your self-realization. Let me put it even more provokingly: I'm after your normality. You're not an earthworm. You're a human being. And so you're normal only when you're constantly developing yourself and realizing your potential.

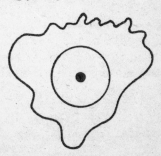

Your normality demands that you constantly observe your inner reality, your inner world, so that it may stay in its perfectly round harmony. Only then are you normal, in your steady self-realization. And then you'll be the 4-Color Person, who, in that 4-ness, achieves the sum total of his or her possibilities. Once again: In the normal human being, the 4-Color Person, the inner circle is round, no matter how twisted the circle of the outer world may be at a given time.

The Infantile Person

However, it's the abnormal things that are generally most frequent. A mishap, stumbling in front of other people, is taken as a personal inadequacy. A refusal is seen as rejection, disgrace, as proof of one's own inferiority.

And vice versa. Some trivial superiority: knowing something that others don't know; the ludicrous possession of the latest fad; a conspicuously loud exhaust on one's car; especially business successes or a calling card with half an alphabet of titles—all these external, overrated successes make the majority of people proud and allegedly "happy." It's as if the external events were crucial for the state of the inner world and a person's self-evaluation.

That's understandable in an infant before the age of three, before his ego has taken shape as an inner world, before he has learned how to think and speak in the first person, the *I*-form.

However, after puberty, parallels between the outer and inner forms indicate a naive failure to distinguish between outer and inner reality.

It is an infantile weakness that contradicts normality. Yet this frequent infantile way of thinking and experiencing is considered "normal" by laymen and experts today.

That, of course, affects our culture. Can you imagine the consequences?

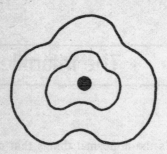

People who believe in God, like Job, maintain the round harmony of their inner circle by trusting in God's reasonable and reliable justice, even if the outer world is shaken by losses and diseases and becomes invalidated. Their weak and irrational egos clutch at God's rationality so that in a misfortune, when feelings inundate thought, they won't short-circuit and confuse inner and outer reality. But what happens when God the Father, together with His rationality, is pensioned off by His modern children? What happens if they fall prey to a new faith, the belief in natural science, in technology, in materialism? What happens when the outer reality is proclaimed as the only reality, as the sole reality that can bring happiness? Who wards off the unthinking confusion between the obvious, external, physical reality and the internal, mental and spiritual reality? You can declare God dead, but the inner reality remains alive and effective all the time.

It's not because the achievement of technology or

the consumption of goods and luxuries are bad. The fact is that the outer reality has been made the golden ideal of happiness by all the shopkeepers in the world, who are interested in mass consumption. And that's why their inner reality—the authentic, ideal, real, experienced happiness—is bankrupt.

You cannot do business with the genuine ideal, with genuine happiness, which is always merely your own very personal inner equilibrium and your self-fulfillment. Your genuine personal happiness is custom-made.

It is naive and infantile to judge inner reality on the basis of outer reality, to assume an internal maturity of character on the basis of external conditions. And yet that false conclusion is reached uncritically by nearly all psychological schools. Alfred Adler, the founder of individual psychology, which was a very valuable achievement, promoted the misunderstanding that feelings of inferiority are caused by physical—that is, external—"organic inferiorities." Although usually an accurate observer, Adler did not distinguish finely enough between an invalid's outer disadvantage and the inner moral judgment.

Amateur psychology, widespread even among professionals, claims that physical disadvantages (a small or unattractive body, a small bosom, baldness, an undesirable shape of the nose, a creaking wooden leg) or the lack of material advantages are the causes of psychological defects.

That fits in beautifully with political materialism. This ideology takes over vulgar pseudoscientific psychology and makes the same claim: Outer reality determines inner reality. Hence, economic disadvantages growing out of the capitalist social system can be the reasons why people feel unhappy or spiritually defective. Proof is offered in the form of external, material, and social conditions (milieu). Such un-sophisticated, incorrect assumptions conveniently ex-cuse all shortcomings in character, form habitual dis-content to criminal aggression. The responsibility is simply put on the milieu, which is just fine with the person in question.

If I throw a rock at a window pane, it will smash. The effect has to follow the cause. In mechanical physics, causality has its unrestricted justification. But this model is false when applied to human beings who can feel themselves as *I*. It is seemingly correct for children, people who react in an infantile manner, and animals to the extent that they respond instinctively and impulsively to outer stimuli.

Anyone examining motives for deeds, especially those of juvenile suicides, will realize that frequently no genuine and comprehensible causes can be found in external reality.

Children with totally different characters and per-sonalities often develop from the same parents, in exactly the same environment, with the very same upbringing. The observer cannot help concluding that these children have been shaped by their special inner worlds, that is to say, their distinct and different self-assessments. It is precisely the ignorance of inner causes, that is to say, of different forms of self-overrating and self-underrating, that leads to the illogi-cal conclusion, the false causal thinking employed in psychological and sociological interpretation.

Now don't misunderstand me. I'm well aware that most people think in those terms and assume about themselves and all others that the inner world is the product of the outer world. But that is a bogus causal-ity, a poor assumption, a misinterpretation, a very serious error in reasoning.

The laws of gravity and a thousand other realities

have always obtained and remained in effect, whether or not they were discovered, known, and developed into a science.

As long as you have no clear ideas and concepts of inner reality, it will remain beyond your ken, hidden in an emotional fog. The person who ignores inner reality is like a blind man who denies the reality of colors because he doesn't know them. The person who disregards the laws and workings of inner reality is like a captain who reckons only with that part of the iceberg that sticks up out of the water. That mistake caused the greatest maritime catastrophe in the history of the world: the sinking of the *Titanic*.

Ignorant of the dynamics of inner reality, laymen and professionals seek refuge in the clichés of external causes, thereby failing to explain internal causes. Any psychological question as to the "why?" triggers instant responses on their part, certain association patterns: only child, insecurity, parents, education, milieu, environmental influences, sex, physical disadvantages. Ramshackle explanations are pieced together out of such catchwords, out of the situations of external reality. These misinterpretations will elicit an "Aha!" from social workers, teachers, ministers, and especially psychologically warped and emotionally amputated mates. Such reasoning, ruthlessly hauled from the drawer of clichés and classifications, makes an impression and arouses quiet admiration—even though it actually fails to illuminate the internal dynamics.

Do you feel I've let off enough steam? That would be great. But I'll be happy if you don't blame your sense of self on the outer world, if I've at least taken you off the *Titanic* course. For then you'll steer along the course of normality. Then you'll be captain of your ship with the four flags: red, green, yellow, and blue.

The Neurotic Personality

Along with the normal personality, whose inner circle remains harmoniously round, and the infantile personality, whose inner circle follows an outer circle, there is also the neurotic personality.

In their childhood, neurotics mostly experienced their milieu as twisted. Since they were naive as children, they imitatively shaped the circle of their inner world with the same warps. Throughout their childhood, they believed they could stand their ground with specific, although distorted, tactics. As a result, the neurotic's inner circle has become fixated in that distortion. The neurotic disorder consists in a fixated and abnormal self-opinion.

In a neurotic adult, the outer world can be, and often is, round and functioning. He or she has a safe roof overhead, a full belly. But the dwarfs and giants inside, the self-underrating and self-overrating, are fighting relentless battles.

Whereas the normal person maintains a round inner world, the adult neurotic does the very opposite, living in a battered inner circle.

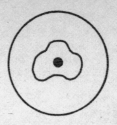

Neurotics with a dented inner life but a fat wallet form the loyal clientele of psychiatrists. For the theme of "I am like this because my environment was like this" is inexhaustible. I feel uncomfortable among neurotics and often bored among infantile people. As a 4-Color Person, you'll be understanding toward both sorts, but your goal is to live as a normal person among normal people.

You may be a wealthy, successful, influential, imaginative, richly emotional average person. But you are normal only if and when you pursue the realization of your *inner* ideal and *inner* model, which are yours and yours alone.

Today, however, the notion of "ideal" is used for any and every need, desire, and buffoonery, from ideal breasts to ideal can openers. So, for the *inner* ideal, which is not a wish but an uncompromising demand (the *conscience*), I prefer the terms *norm* and *normality*.

Normal or Average?

Recently I was talking about the latest kidnapping. "Anarchists who commit such terrorist acts are not normal," said someone who was visibly indignant.

"If the kidnappers aren't normal, then they're not responsible for their actions. Where would that leave us?" said someone else. Soon came the cardinal question which is always asked in these situations but never answered: "Who *is* really normal?"

One of the daily tasks of many psychiatrists is to decide whether the patient is suffering from mental conflicts and disorders (a *neurosis*) which afflict normal people, or whether there is also an abnormality, a so-called mental disease (a *psychosis*)—for instance, schizophrenia.

If a psychiatrist has to express an expert opinion in court, a judgment must be made as to whether a culprit has committed a crime as a "normal" person or as someone "not responsible for his or her actions." If the culprit was drunk, psychotic, or feebleminded, then the conclusion is that he or she was not normally responsible.

I do not assume that you doubt your normality. But I'm sure you occasionally ask yourself: "What would be the best thing for me to do now? What would be the normal solution to my problem?"

Have you ever wondered what *normal* means? It is easier to establish that unsuitable or absurd behavior is abnormal than to explain what is really normal.

What I find confusing is that *normal* and *average* are so similar that both concepts are sometimes used synonymously. At the same time, everything in me is up in arms at the idea of accepting as normal only what the average run of humanity does. Most people lead a life full of internal compulsions and arduously played roles. That is not what I can regard as a normal life.

Normal and *average,* which I would like to keep apart, always keep overlapping. Supposedly, the loss of vision is a normal process of old age. But is blindness per se normal? Certainly not, although a blind man as a human being is normal. Is a brain-damaged young girl normal? She is usually unable to learn how to read or write. Nevertheless, she may be highly sensitive to relationships. Is a clever businessman normal even when he is so inhumane that we have to speak of an abnormal lack of feeling? He is then comparable to an "unfeeling psychopath," who likewise has no sympathy, sense of honor, justice, or sense of shame. If people's thoughts or actions are deeply altered by sickness or advanced age, are they still normal? Or should we no longer take them seriously because they "don't quite know what they're saying"?

You have probably often noticed that very many people stop being honest if they can obtain an apparently important advantage or if honesty could be damaging. Nevertheless, neither parents nor spouses would regard dishonesty toward one another or toward others as a normal attitude.

In the realm of technology, people speak about norms in reference to units of measurement and measurable quantities. Here, what is normal is standardized.

Accordingly, we say that the physical size of a dwarf or a giant deviates from the norm as an average.

But don't you feel that Johann Sebastian Bach, Albert Einstein, and Goethe deviated from the average through their intellectual achievements and yet were perfectly normal? Here, evidently, *normal* has nothing to do with *average*. Normality is actually measured by how true, how genuine, how realistic a person's perception and behavior are.

You judge behavior as normal or say that a person is "very normal" if behavior is proper to a situation. However, in order to act normal and according to the outer reality, you have to have a standard, that is, specific norms, to go by. Such standard norms are the internal ideals, which, as spiritual values, point out your way. These are ideals you go by in order to judge and behave correctly.

Psychiatrists and sociologists employ such inner ideals and norms to determine a person's normality. If a mother didn't have the ideal of caring for her children, she wouldn't be normal. If a grown man didn't have the ideal of caring for himself, eating on his own, walking on his own, achieving things on his own, he wouldn't be normal. A man who really had no inner ideals whatsoever would not be normal.

Hence, *normal* means two things.

In all physical and technological areas, *normal* means *standard, average*. Here, the norm is the *average norm*.

However, its meaning is radically different when it refers to a spiritual value, an inner ideal. The inner ideal as a norm has nothing to do with the average multitude. *Quantity* and *average* play no part here. Whether or not people are honest on the average, honesty toward others remains an inner ideal, a norm to orient normal people in their speech and behavior.

If you have to deal professionally with psychological statistics, then I feel you ought to think about their limits. Since normality is an ideal and not an average value, it cannot, by its very definition, be computed in quantitative or statistical terms. Statistical average values thus provide only sociological information. They permit no insights into the normal structure of the human psyche or into the psychological structure of a specific individual.

The normality determining the psychological judgment of and counseling for healthy or conflict-ridden neurotic people can and must be measured only by qualitatively defined ideal-norms. If, however, you insist on judging an individual person according to statistically computed tables, then you can cover your hollow head with the skipper's cap of a *Titanic* psychologist.

Ideals, Yes; Ideologies, No

Inner ideals are a necessity for you and for every person who asks about the meaning of life. You ask about the meaning that your life has as a whole. If ideals are to represent this integral meaning, they must show all possibilities of social self-realization. Thus, the ideals of inner reality are also norms. Like internal guideposts, they point out only the direction that a person should take. Inner ideals are thus by no means "goals" that we can attain. They indicate directions and they help us find our bearings. The more consistently you live in terms of these inner ideals, the more normal you are. the more authentically natural, and the further you move from the average of our society, which is fixated in abnormal roles and unnatural compulsions. Since the "meaning of life" covers the full range of the possibilities of human life, any absolute, one-sided ideal—that is, every ideology—is absurd. In anarchistic terrorism, as in other ideologies that include a thirst for power, this absurdity has a tragic consequence: the negation of all other ideals, especially tolerance, and the destruction of existing values.

Intolerance thus is an essential part of any ideology. For no matter how many forms reality takes, no matter how frequently it changes, any ideology constantly interprets reality in terms of an absolute, unilateral ideal. Using this principle, the followers of the ideology think they can explain and overcome anything. Anarchists, for instance—assuming they are not conflict-ridden, aggressive people—have an absolute ideal of "social justice." They scorn other social ideals, such as tolerance, openmindedness, sincerity, kindness, benevolence. And so they negate all other ideals and battle against their application. That is why ideologies, even scientific and artistic ones, are intolerant. Political and religious ideologies in particular, because of their power demands, are usually destructive as well.

Young people ask about the meaning of life and expect some answer describing how life should be lived. With this question, young people are all too easily taken in by the simplistic interpretations of ideologists.

A lot of people, in their youth, adhered to "ideals" and were ultimately disillusioned—for instance, many followers of Nazism, communism, or other political or religious ideologies. Such people have thrown these so-called ideals and the attendant idealism overboard and now consider themselves "sober realists" (thereby falling victim to another ideology). Having ideals, being an idealist, sounds naive and ridiculous to such people. But in their disappointment, they have never come to realize that they failed to orient themselves on genuine inner ideals. They merely pursued an ideology.

An Interim Balance

I feel it's time we drew a balance. I hope you don't mind if we now reflect on what we've achieved.

Thinking back to what's been discussed, what is the first thing you recall? What comes to mind? Mull it over, but take your time. What is the first point for you? Does anything else cross your mind? Was something else important to you? What is the second point that was new or essential for you?

Let's ask from the opposite perspective. Is any facet missing? What else would you like to learn about the 4-Color Person? What still prevents you from becoming a 4-Color Person and enjoying life to the hilt?

I have asked you what aspects were so important for you as to result in some practical profit. However, I'm perfectly willing to be asked in exchange: "What do you consider important among all the things you've told us?"

The bike parable is important for me. If I'm annoyed about something or if I don't know whether to get my way or turn to more pleasurable tasks, or even if I'm sitting on the horns of a dilemma, or if the fear of death sneaks up on me, then I know I've fallen off the bicycle seat. Then I know that I haven't kept my balance or that I've fallen into a passive self-pity.

It was also worthwhile realizing clearly that I have to distinguish between external reality and internal reality. I know even more clearly today that an external mishap must not, under any circumstances, influence my sense of self.

And vice versa: I know that external successes, whether fame or money, which flatter me and reassure me, must have absolutely no influence on my inner world, on my true sense of self. If an external success were to make me arrogant and immodest, then I would have to quote Matthew: "For what profiteth it a man if he shall gain the whole world and lose his own soul?"

I understand that I always have to strive for the four senses of self (self-respect, self-confidence, self-moderation, self-development) in order to achieve inner harmony, what I've called normality. That insight made me realize, in turn, what self-guidance and harmonious self-realization are.

For me, the four colors are symbols (archetypes) of the four kinds of senses of self and of thought and action. I often call myself to account:

Do I live in terms of *red*, like Robinson Crusoe, so that I acquire enough self-confidence?

Do I live in terms of *blue*, like Diogenes, so that I feel contented in self-moderation?

Do I live in terms of *green*, like a nobleman, so that I can respect myself because I stick to my convictions?

Do I live in terms of *yellow*, like Hans-in-Luck, so that I can develop new possibilities?

The daily joy and cheer, the wealth of versatile and intensely experienced hours, are a certificate for me that no university and no ordained priest can bestow. I cannot hang it up on the wall as a skilled 4-Color Person. But I feel it within me and I am happy and grateful for it.

The Ethics of the 4-Color Person

If you do everything you can to feel really good, then others will also profit from that.

If you realize and balance your four normal senses of self, then you'll be a pleasant partner for other people—if for no other reason than because you refrain from doing what other people can't stand. But, even for your own sake, you do a lot of things that other people like and from which they profit greatly.

The 4-Color Person may be Epicurus or Shakespeare, Dick or Jane. No matter who he or she is, the lackey morality—"You shouldn't . . . you mustn't"—strikes that person as a playpen for moral infants. Four-Color People are independent because—and so long as—they maintain their equilibrium. Being independent, they feel free, even though they live in a specific society and belong to a specific civilization. You've read right: They feel free. They are not puppets, and they don't hang on any ideological apron strings—whether of theological divinities, state-controlled lawmakers, or even rebellion-oriented leftists. They are neither the underlings of a state, nor the lackeys of a church, a society, or a mate. Instead, they support them because—and to the extent that—they are useful, so long as their conviction is congruent with their goals. For whatever you do in terms of your own conviction and responsibility will not be left by you as a compulsion. you realize your freedom by doing what you feel is right.

Previously only very few people, and only with the instinct of an inspired sovereignty, succeeded in realizing a morality that the 4-Color Person achieves with crystal-clear understanding and independent conviction: the morality of acting in terms of what is suitable for the conscience.

As I said before, two hundred years ago Immanuel Kant formulated his categorical imperative as a universal principle of ethics: Act in such a way that the maxims of your behavior can always serve simultaneously as a universal legislation. For 4-Color People, that is the logical bridge from their inner world to their outer world, from their thought to their action, from their inner equilibrium to a social, ethical responsibility.

The categorical imperative is our bridge from inside to outside, from the normal senses of self to social behavior.

For the sake of thoroughness, I want to remind you that we have arrived at the following four senses of self (their logical foundations are in Part Four of this book):

YELLOW	RED
Freedom	Self-realization
Self-development	Self-confidence
BLUE	**GREEN**
Self-contentment	Self-determination
Self-moderation	Self-respect

Daily behavior frequently combines two senses of self. The six possible combinations from certain familiar moods and states in how we feel about ourselves.

Two examples:

From the green field of "self-respect" and the blue field of "self-moderation" comes: seriousness.

From the red field of "self-confidence" in connection with the yellow field of "freedom, self-development" comes: cheerfulness, serenity.

The Basic Ethical Norms

JUSTICE   AQUA MARINE

A man who strives to make decisions in terms of his convictions (green) and adjusts modestly to the given possibilities (blue)—that man is serious (green and blue). He acts justly toward others.

By using the example of justice, I would like to show you, step by step, how we arrive at the philosophical-scientific definition of the basic ethical norm of "justice."

Self-respect comes about through "honest conviction." The same man as above who moderates himself, who sticks to what is real and actual and comes to terms with the given possibilities, is honest and modest; he is serious. According to the categorical imperative, we need merely translate that sense of self into an action. It will then correspond to justice. The categorical imperative turns the sense of self that we call "seriousness" into a basic ethical norm: justice, proper behavior based on reality, fairness.

Hence (green and blue): Ego norm: serious. Social norm: justice.

OPEN-MINDEDNESS ORANGE

A woman who feels free and independent (yellow) and also has confidence in her strength and ability (red)—that woman is serene (yellow and red). She is open-minded toward others (her social attitude), and she is sympathetic to their needs. The two senses of self—self-development (yellow) and self-confidence (red)—thus produce the social attitude and the basic ethical norm that we call open-mindedness and sympathy.

This attitude is not something we can take for granted. There is the grouchy husband who uses his newspaper as a screen or the successful businessman who likes ideas only if he's been familiar with them since childhood or if he comes up with them himself. Those men are breaking the eleventh commandment: "Thou shalt not be closed-minded."

Hence (yellow and red): Ego norm: serenity. Social norm: open, sympathetic mind.

RESPONSIBILITY BROWN

People who make decisions out of honest convictions, who have a solid and genuine sense of their own worth (green) and at the same time confidence in their strength and ability (red)—those people are sure of themselves (green and red).

The self-assured person does not cop out. Nor are such people weak or yielding. They are ready to take responsibility and, if they consider it right, to offer help, relying on conviction (green) and on confidence in their own strength (red).

If they act according to the categorical imperative and translate their feeling of self-assurance into social behavior, they are being helpful and responsible. We call this basic ethical norm *helpful responsibility*.

Hence (green and red): Ego norm: self-assurance. Social norm: helpful responsibility.

TOLERANCE   *GREEN*

People who adjust out of moderation (blue) and yet feel free and independent (yellow) are those happy, carefree people who never worry unnecessarily. If people have a carefree sense of self, they act tolerant toward others. Tolerant people are ready to work with others. They are cooperative because they have no authoritarian power claims. They are also willing to be considerate, to make responsible compromises, and they know that an agreement with the legitimate interests of others should be striven for.

Hence (yellow and blue): Ego norm: carefree. Social norm: tolerance.

SINCERITY   *LIGHT GREEN*

Sincerity presumes that a person feels self-reliant. Someone under the pressure of dependence, for instance a child, who has to fear punishment and lack of sympathy, will hardly be sincere.

Self-reliance is a combination of two senses of self: independence (yellow) and honest conviction (green). People who have these senses of self, who feel self-reliant, without material, sexual, or ideological dependence—those people can be sincere and honest in their social behavior. Only such people are credible.

Hence (yellow and green): Ego norm: self-reliance. Social norm: sincerity.

BENEVOLENCE   *PURPLE*

Wishing someone well is a sign of goodness or genuine love. Kind love and benevolence presume an inner state of contentment.

Contentment is a combination of two senses of self: on the one hand, self-moderation, the willingness to adjust to the given possibilities (blue); and on the other hand, self-confidence (red). People can be truly content only if they have confidence in their strength and abilities.

Using the example of this last basic ethical norm, kind benevolence, I would like to show you once again that the sense of self as the inner reality produces ethical behavior—through the categorical imperative —as the outer reality:

Confidence in one's own strength and self-moderation, those two senses of self, create the state of contentment. Contentment, in turn, through the categorical imperative, leads to a kind and benevolent attitude toward others.

Hence (blue and red): Ego norm: content. Social norm: kind benevolence.

Deriving the Ego Norms and the Social Norms

The four normal senses of self are called ego norms:

> Self-respect (green)
> Self-confidence (red)
> Self-moderation (blue)
> Self-development (yellow)

They combine to form six further senses of self or ego norms:

> Serene
> Serious
> Self-assured
> Carefree
> Self-reliant
> Content

These six ego norms, through the categorical imperative, produce the six social norms (the basic ethical norms).

EGO NORM		CATEGORICAL IMPERATIVE	SOCIAL NORM
Self-respect Self-moderation	serious	produces	justice
Self-development Self-confidence	serene	produces	open-mindedness
Self-confidence Self-respect	self-assured	produces	responsibility
Self-development Self-moderation	carefree	produces	tolerance
Self-respect Self-development	self-reliant	produces	sincerity
Self-moderation Self-confidence	content	produces	kind benevolence

The Basic Ethical Norms and the Ten Commandments

In regard to the substance of what I've been describing, the relationship to the Judeo-Christian commandments is obvious. "Thou shalt not bear false witness" is a demand for sincerity. However, our basic ethical norm of sincerity is much more comprehensive. Not lying and not misleading are merely part of sincerity. A relationship is truly sincere only if one unreservedly tells the other anything of concern; for instance, that one has fallen in love with someone else.

The commandment "Thou shalt not steal" is a demand for justice. But the norm of justice is again far more comprehensive than the commandment not to steal. Any profit to someone else's disadvantage is unjust. Justice requires fair play as a basic attitude. People who do not stick to facts, who defend themselves with poor arguments and rationalizations, are likewise unjust.

The tolerant person kills no one merely for belonging to a different race, a different political or religious conviction. Once again, tolerance in its full scope is far more comprehensive than the commandment "Thou shalt not kill." True tolerance is respect and appreciation of the right to be different. If people, in different living conditions, have different modes of behavior, that does not reduce or affect their human dignity. Intolerance is the expression of arrogant power or arrogant high-handedness and limited intelligence.

The ethical norm of kind and loving benevolence is expressed in the commandment "Thou shalt honor thy father and mother." It would seem that genuine love did not always play the important role that we now assign to it. Unfortunately, this role is often merely *played*. So, in the next section, I would like to talk to you about genuine love.

The basic ethical norms of the 4-Color Person are not formulated defensively like the Ten Commandments—"Thou shalt not. . . ." Instead, our ethics fundamentally command: Thou shalt have an open mind. How much different the importance and history of the Christian church would have been if it had known and applied this commandment!

I have explained the six basic ethical norms in my book *Signals of Personality*. Furthermore, in that book, I have described self-realization in contrast to inauthentic role behavior, the way the red type, the blue type, the green type, and the yellow type dress, the kinds of ornaments they wear, the expressions they use, their hobbies and vices, and the way they furnish their homes.

Genuine Love

Of the six basic ethical norms, kind benevolence is the most important prerequisite for genuine love. But sincerity and justice and helpful responsibility likewise make a partnership into genuine love. Tolerance and open-mindedness similarly are signs of a genuine, loving relationship.

The statement "Love Thy neighbor as thyself" strikes me as a mathematical equation: Love your neighbor to the extent that you are capable of finding genuine love for yourself. But how do you find genuine love for yourself? What does it consist of? This difficult question is already solved for us. Genuine love for yourself consists of realizing for yourself the four senses of self: self-respect, self-confidence, self-moderation, and self-development.

"Loving oneself" thus means striving for and realizing the normal senses of self.

If you transfer this love, this harmonious sense of self, to your neighbor, if you are benevolent, sincere, just, helpful, tolerant, and open-minded toward that person, they you have formed a loving relationship.

So it makes sense to say: "If you don't love your-self, you can't love others."

I think it would be worthwhile, after these clarifying insights, to discuss a fundamental theme of our lives: love, or more precisely, our self-realization in love. We usually have more capacity for success, wealth, or business than we do for genuine love. The fault lies in our education and upbringing. For many, "love" is computed like a business deal, as an exchange of one's own consumer value (beauty, youth, intelligence, property, sex, attractiveness, background, social pres-tige) for a partner's consumer value. People who compute or "feel" like that do not love. They are merely impressed by the role that their partners con-stitute for them. They admire those advantages in their partners (beauty, intelligence, social prestige, prop-erty) that they themselves would like to have. When people seek and find impressive those things that they actually wish for themselves, then they are "in love." They believe they have found true love. But that has nothing to do with genuine love, with truly great love. Even worse, that kind of being "in love" is an obstacle to genuine love.

The things that people would like to be or aspire to, the things they lack themselves—those things are what they hope to get from their partners. The hoped-for profit may come. But love never comes, and it is replaced by disappointment. If people don't resign themselves to their disappointment, they try to draw their profit from new partners. This merely brings a new disappointment. The lonelier and, hence, the more demanding people become, the more "love"-starved they feel. They often indulge in sexual excesses as an attempt to anesthetize the depressing lack of contact and love. If sexuality is masturbation by means of the partner or the aggressive subjugation of the partner, it can easily deteriorate into dependency and jealousy. But such sex is not great and genuine love. Nor is passion as sexual dependency a sign of genuine love. With genuine love, in contrast, sex is always an expression of sensitive rapport and intimacy in all their varieties.

Freud, the great psychologist and researcher of sex, scarcely touched a chief theme of psychology: love. His disciple Theodor Reik, and especially Erich Fromm and more recent psychologists, have written essential treatments, giving love its deserved importance in psychology. But among some psychiatrists and laymen under Freud's influence, there is still a gross confusion of love and "satisfaction of the sexual drives." The love of the heart is seen as merely a "sublimation" of the frustrated sexual instinct, a kind of detour from a closed street.

If genuine love, true love, is no longer a transaction in the consumer's market of supply and demand, then the question is not "How can I find true love and someone who loves me absolutely?" The question becomes "How am I capable of great love?" For the experience of great love implies an ability for genuine love.

What the partner is like is of secondary importance. Of primary importance is: "What must I be like to love genuinely?"

Only a minority of people fulfill the conditions for genuine love. For most people, great love remains an illusion throughout their lives because they have never mastered that art. Without knowing the ideals of love, the art of love cannot be learned. Psychologists who believe in Freud's sexualization do not know these ideals.

Theologians with their sanctimonious embarrassment about sex and their moralistic opposition to sensuousness are nothing but sexually amputated preachers of love. For love without sensuousness and tenderness is as empty as a musical score without the musicians.

Even love songs are questionable teachers for the ideals of love. The pop lyrics that fill our ears with love every day sound utterly stupid, Yet the tritest things, "stars" and "eternity," have the deeper meaning that ideals (stars) give permanence (eternity) to true love.

A dissatisfied person may need love, would like to be loved, but is not ready for genuine love. Contentment can be learned. It pre-supposes on the one hand self-moderation and adjustment (naturally not subjugation) and on the other hand self-confidence, confidence in one's own strength.

This answer will surprise those people who are looking for an "ideal partner," for genuine love arises through the ideals of self-realization. On the one hand, ideals are inner conditions—self-confidence and modesty. On the other hand, they are ways of acting toward the partner: tolerance, helpfulness, sincerity, and, above all, a kind benevolence. But these preconditions are hard to master, because suitable models do not expose the private world of their genuine love. The images of people we are presented with—for example, the newscaster or a popular singer—are not models. Nevertheless, in publicity, stars are presented as models on TV and in newspapers and magazines, because (and this is also the goal) the public admires them.

Such people are often very immodest, even when acting patronizingly modest toward the public. It is a sure sign of immodesty and lack of love when so-called celebrities feed the gossip columns with their intimate private lives and when their autobiographies actually document that they are incapable of intimacy, which most people protect against strangers.

In a society where everything, even the learned behavior of intimacy, plays an impressive role, modesty atrophies, and, with it, authenticity and the ability to love are likewise stunted.

In a society where everything is aimed at impressing others, one can easily become pompous. Such people are not capable of love. For they do everything—often astonishingly useful things—for their self-assurance. And even in their most intimate encounters, they are intent on having an effect. The person who plays the role of helplessness and self-pity is equally incapable of genuine love. The role of weepy helplessness—"I can't live without you!"—is often used by women as a manipulative tactic or a childlike attitude with the corresponding intonation.

Both pompous self-assurance and childish helplessness are roles used to exert an authoritarian influence on the other person. They stunt any development of normal self-confidence. Yet confidence in one's own strength and a helpful attitude are among the major prerequisites for the ability to love.

In a society in which prestige and a pompous effort to impress are so important, a necessary modesty is ill appreciated.

By being prepared to adjust and to modify exaggerated demands out of consideration for the partner, people develop a feeling of togetherness, the kind of relationship that one wishes for—a genuine love. Immoderation, on the other hand, is often a reason for the failure of love relationships.

Many men think they are playing their role correctly if they act overbearing and immoderate.

In a misunderstood emancipation, many women

today are imitating that inauthentic male role. They think it's emancipated to behave as immoderately as men do. Instead of a real emancipation, instead of a real liberation, these women take on the constraint of an imitated male role.

Moderation, the prerequisite for contentment and an ability to love, means adjustment, but not subservience or sacrifice. The person who confuses helpfulness with self-sacrifice is guilty of self-abandonment, self-denial. Helpfulness and love expect no reward. But people who "sacrifice" themselves are secretly calculating, for they demand gratitude and some kind of recompense.

Every good deed that comes from a feeling of sacrifice does not arise from either moderation or genuine love. Self-denial is an authoritarian role, with which one tries to force love or gratitude and dependency ("I'll do anything for you so that you'll love me."). Nor can love be forced through self-denial. Such compulsion springs from immoderation, and it kills love.

Most of all, immoderation expresses itself in the often tacit demands one makes on a partner. One frequently requires an excess of constant attention or an excess of acknowledgment. At times, the demand to be spoiled is exaggerated. Or else one forces one's own way with ruthless egoism. All these immoderate expectations lead to disappointments and soon to resentment of the partner. Symptoms of the inner rejection of the partner are hypersensitivity, critical willfulness, reservations, nagging or cold silence, and reproachful defiance. The defensiveness increases into an inner freeze against the partner and into sexual indifference or rejection. The consequences of immoderation are, first, aloofness, then isolation, and finally separation.

Genuine moderation and genuine self-confidence are thus prerequisites for a fulfilled harmonious love relationship. There is a further ideal, the ideal of inner self-reliance, that is one of the guiding rules of love. A person who feels dependent on material, sexual or social demands will cling to a partner for security. The person who "loves" out of dependency, or remains tied to someone for that reason, will never find true love. The person who feels dependent can neither live in terms of real conviction, nor be open and sincere toward a partner. The person who has not become inwardly self-reliant will remain unfree, living in a dependency that creates hatred and kills all love.

At this point, I do not want to list the countless deformations of love, the sexual, material, and social attitudes of profit and frustration. I simply want to demonstrate the internal prerequisites that make a person ready for great, genuine love. Nevertheless, we can answer the secondary question: "Who would be the right partner for true love?"

The right partner is the person who has those same characteristics and is likewise capable of love, who has learned the art of loving according to the ideals of self-reliance and contentment, self-confidence and moderation, and who therefore acts tolerant and helpful, sincere and open-minded toward the partner.

Great, genuine love is no illusion. But many people never experience it, and most people experience it only briefly and partially. For love is an art that must be learned and, like any art, practiced and performed.

The ideals demonstrated here (self-moderation and self-confidence, and kind benevolence out of inner contentment, as well as sincerity, helpful responsibility, and tolerance) are necessary prerequisites for a genuine and harmonious love relationship.

You can take these ideals as a checklist. Using it,

you can check your attitude toward the other person and your way of dealing with him or her, especially the way you speak.

Great love is experienced not just as a sexual partnership, but as an authentic togetherness. It is a mutual complement, forming a whole. It is an essential part of self-realization. In genuine togetherness, the partners may have different interests and opinions, which they mutually tolerate. But they always agree with their ideals. That—and only that—requires total agreement. A partnership in which this ideal of agreement becomes mutual experience and certainty is true love, genuine love. That rapport is authentic intimacy.

Checklist and Guidelines
for Inner Balance

If your car is out of order, you can take it to a mechanic. If your inner balance is out of kilter, you can go to the psychiatrist. But unlike the mechanic who can fix your car, the psychiatrist cannot repair your balance. That's your job. Think of the bicycle parable. At best, the psychiatrist can offer you guidance on how you can restore your equilibrium.

The handbooks for cars or household appliances contain instructions on where to look for the causes of disorders. Likewise, you can use a checklist as a practical guide for the possible causes of disorders in your senses of self or the resulting conflicts.

I do not have the illusion that this can cure neurotic character developments. But if you're mentally healthy and have any difficulties that you would like to understand and resolve, if you have conflicts with your partner, if you have worries, are suffering from loneliness or a bitter disappointment, or if you intend to become or remain a 4-Color Person, then this checklist and the accompanying guidelines can be helpful to you.

You may find typical abnormal attitudes of yours in the following checklist. You may be suffering from problems or conflicts (or you may recognize yourself on the color wheel and among the types discussed in Part Two). If so, then you can check under the corresponding type (e.g., A., the good-natured angel, or 1., the dissatisfied devil) and find the guideline to show you how to change your inner attitude.

To make the guideline effective when worries or annoyances throw you off balance, you should review it over and over again. Review it everywhere: while falling asleep and waking up, in autogenic training, in a car, at a desk, or when looking into a mirror. Review it until it becomes a part of you.

Dale Carnegie, one of the great practical psychologists, said that one of his many recipes for dealing with worries and problems was the following:

1. Write down the things that worry or disturb you. Establish the facts accurately.
2. Analyze the facts. Ask yourself what would be the worst thing that could happen.
3. Ask yourself what you can do about it.
4. Make a decision and fix a time for carrying it out.

Furthermore, I owe Dale Carnegie the following quotations, which I would like to put at the head of the checklist:

Montaigne: "Man does not suffer as much from the things that happen to him as from the way he reacts to them."

Marcus Aurelius: "Our life is what our thoughts make it."

Abraham Lincoln: "Most people are about as happy as they intend to be."

For the man who is not a Hans-in-Luck, Seneca

advises: "Start to live now and count every day as a life in itself."

THE BLUE CHECKLIST

Is self-moderation fulfilled?
Are you a Diogenes? Do you adjust to the given possibilities?
Or are you a good-natured angel?
Is self-sacrifice your weakness?

a. Do you sacrifice yourself for someone because you believe you can thereby obtain his or her love?
b. Do you admire others (prestigious people) to make them like you?
c. Do you simulate feelings and likings to get others to like you? Is your emotional response merely a tactical maneuver?
d. Do you suppress your true feelings in order not to hurt others or to keep them from disliking you?
e. Are you so yielding that you sacrifice yourself to others who exploit you?

If you have answered several of these questions with *yes*, then I would advise you to take the following guideline for your inner equilibrium:
Instead of sacrificing myself and denying my true claims, I will make my demands and be prepared to take the consequences if the demands are not fruitful.
Are you a dissatisfied devil?
Is dissatisfaction with yourself your weakness?

a. Do you feel that other people don't understand you, but that you yourself contribute too little to making them understand you better and bringing about harmony?

b. Do you feel you can't trust anybody and can't rely on anybody, yet you avoid having it out?

c. Do you lack a feeling of trustful togetherness, yet you won't empathize with patience and understanding?

If you have answered several of these questions with *yes*, then I would advise you to take the following guideline for your inner equilibrium:
I will summon up more loving patience and understanding and I will work at the relationship so that it satisfies me instead of turning away when something bothers me.

THE GREEN CHECKLIST

Is self-respect fulfilled?
Are you a nobleman? Do you live according to your honest conviction?
Or are you a conceited peacock?
Is overrating yourself your weakness?

a. Do you make yourself the prisoner of your authority role and your demand for esteem?

b. Are you a victim of your success, your beauty, your property, your intelligence, your fine background, or some other privilege that makes you conceited and that you still haven't come to terms with?

c. Are you a know-it-all or do you show off with critical reservations?

If you have answered several of these questions with *yes*, then I would advise you to take the following guideline for your inner equilibrium:

I will adjust and conform to the given possibilities instead of withdrawing into my false pride.

Or are you an agile snake?

Are self-doubts your weakness?

a. Are you dependent on praise and reproach, are you taken in by the advantages of prestige?
b. Do you lack the courage to be yourself, do you flee into fads and adopt a pseudo-personality?
c. Do you put things off till tomorrow when you know that you have to make a decision right here and now?
d. Do you flee into pretexts to avoid decision and action?
e. Are you willing to give up things in order to achieve what you realize is necessary?

If you have answered several of these questions with *yes,* then I would advise you to take the following guideline for your inner equilibrium:

I realize I have futile demands and I will make up my mind either to give them up or to do what is necessary for myself.

THE RED CHECKLIST

Is self-confidence fulfilled?

Are you a Robinson Crusoe? Do you apply your physical and mental abilities and capabilities? Do you say, "I'll give it a try?" Do you have the courage to take risks?

Or are you a pompous braggart and do you ask too much of yourself?

Is overconfidence your weakness?

a. Are you a pompous fool, boring others with your achievements, your sexual prowess, or your name-dropping?
b. Do you boast about having no time?
c. Do you brag and boast with your clothing, an attractive mate, your home, your titles?
d. Do you try to show your sexual mate that you are a good lover?

If you have answered several of these questions with *yes*, then I would advise you to take the following guideline for your inner equilibrium:
I will try to figure out calmly the things that are really important for me instead of trying to impress others and indulging in expensive bragging or perilous risks.
Or are you a tormented martyr?
Is self-pity your weakness?

a. Do you pass the buck to others? Do you blame your discomfort on other people or circumstances and relish your self-pity?
b. Have you made yourself dependent on your mate or on your professional situation and do you regard that as a reason for pitying yourself?
c. Do you prefer to be helped and do you lay claim to charity from others when you could just as easily do something yourself?

If you have answered several of these questions with *yes*, then I would advise you to take the following guideline for your inner equilibrium:
I will not accept any condition under which I will suffer permanently. Instead of wallowing in self-pity, I will try to reach my goal with my own strength.

THE YELLOW CHECKLIST

Are self-development, inner dependence, and freedom fulfilled?
Are you a Hans-in-Luck? Do you realize your possibilities?
Or are you a dreamer full of expectations?
Is illusionary flight from yourself your weakness?

a. Do you escape into daydreams while knowing that you will not seriously have any of these wishes come true?
b. Would you like to earn a lot of money with little work and have a lot of things without giving up other things that you like?
c. Do you tend toward wishful thinking, and do you talk yourself into believing that everything will turn out as you wish? Do you do that especially at times when you are actually unsure and full of doubts?

If you have answered several of these questions with *yes*, then I would advise you to take the following guideline for your inner equilibrium:
I will determine whether I am chasing rainbows and fooling myself about my inner state of dissatisfaction instead of merely trying to put it in order.
Or are you a defensive knight in armor?
Is self-constraint your weakness?

a. Are you a prisoner of your false prestige worship: "What will other people say?"
b. Do you lack the courage to feel your wishes, express them, and act in accordance with them?
c. Are you dependent on acknowledgment by others or on your self-assurance, and do you feel you have

to constantly prove your worth with special successes or accomplishments?

d. Are you upset by a bitter disappointment or do you suffer from jealousy, envy, and hence become vengeful instead of being a Hans-in-Luck, saying goodbye to loss and worry, and opening yourself up to new pleasures?

e. Do you compulsively feel you have to emulate a model of success or virtue instead of doing your best, independently, and being yourself?

f. Do you depend on assurance from others and are you upset by unfair criticism instead of seeing it as envy and secret recognition?

If you have answered several of these questions with *yes*, then I would advise you to take the following guideline for your inner equilibrium:

I will not put any inner compulsion upon myself and I will not exceed my own personal demands, but I will remain open to all possibilities and take advantage of the right ones.

2

THE NON-4-COLOR
PERSON

Goal Tactics And Defense Tactics

It's as clear as day that there are two kinds of people: the normal and the other kind. The 4-Color People are in the first group, and everyone else belongs to the second.

Since you consider yourself normal, we can talk openly about the others. They deviate from the norm. They feel like either inferior dwarfs or superior giants. If you look *through* them and not merely *at* them as they play their roles, you realize that each giant contains an anxiety-ridden dwarf and each dwarf an arrogant giant. Anyone who acts important, needs to. Inside, however, such people feel like gnomes.

Only a normal individual, only the 4-Color Person, shows his or her true face. All others exhibit a Janus head with a front and a back side. The front side is a pose to teach you what you're supposed to think about them—that they're superior, self-assured, rich, intelligent, popular or loving, tender, solicitous or charming, attractive, romantic, imaginative, and erotically promising. A pose is a tactic to impress or influence others in a specific way and to attain a desired goal.

But every front side has a back side. If a man has a front side of a pompous show-off, indicating how much he has to do and how little time he has, and documenting his importance and responsibility with outbursts of anger—that man has a mental as well as an anatomical back side. And the mental back side reveals the very opposite of his front side. It reveals the reason for his peculiar behavior. The man who is pursuing a goal with a specific pose is secretly trying to ward off a specific cause, a specific undesirable situation.

People who emphasize their importance by means of anger or by saying "I have no time . . . I have all the responsibility" fear they are not being taken seriously or they don't feel up to the situation. Inside, they regard themselves as spineless puppets and tormented martyrs. The top manager who merges concerns the way his wife cracks eggs into a pan may feel helplessly at the mercy of his wife's tormenting nagging—the result of her sense of unimportance next to him. If he then whispers in a comforting voice, "Darling, you need relaxation as much as I do," then the superman has slipped into the role of the spineless puppet. He submits, so as not to have to deal with his wife's authoritarian nagging. That too is a tactic for warding off an undesirable situation.

Tactics are sometimes necessary. You and I and others are going to form some kind of defense against an undesirable situation. We try to find ways and means to deal with it. From now on, let's call this attitude a *defense tactic*.

Sometimes it's practical to find ways and means to create a desirable situation. From now on, let's call this intention a *goal tactic*.

If need be, you make use of a tactic and you wield the foil with a light hand. Precisely because your self-realization consists in dealing and being in harmony with reality, it is sometimes useful to apply a well-considered defense tactic or a far-sighted goal tactic.

Thus there are three different kinds of situations:

1. As a 4-Color Person, you are in harmony with reality and are filled with the situation. You agree with it. As a 4-Color Person, you have a feeling of harmony in a tender sensuous experience, in a dialogue filled with wonder, on a well-controlled horse, or on skis in the balletic swaying of your body.
2. You are dissatisfied with the situation. You reject it. You resist with a suitable defense tactic.
3. You wish for a different and better situation. You pursue it with a suitable goal tactic.

Since you have the proper measure, the norm of the 4-Color Person, before your eyes, you put aside the shield of your defense tactic and the arrow of your goal tactic as quickly as possible and you return to your beloved equilibrium (=). That's how the 4-Color Person acts. But not the average person. The average person remains an incorrigible complainer, an unfairly treated hyena or a sad sack of self-pity. The defense against unwished-for situations in life becomes a fixated attitude toward life, a neurotic defense.

Every back side has a front side, every defense tactic has a goal tactic. That is why average people squander their time proving that they are the most important grain of sand in the desert of human society. They strive to attract attention as dwarf celebrities, to make themselves popular at parties, to burden themselves with impressive property, to fill out their empty days with honorary offices, to gain status as interesting personalities with extravagant hobbies, or furnish castles in the air during long sessions of daydreaming.

All these life tactics, the defense tactics against undesirable situations and the goal tactics for creating desirable situations, will now be described for you precisely. In this way, you can see through them quickly when you encounter them in everyday life.

The Typology of the Non-4-Color Person

What we are after is nothing less than a typology of all non-4-Color People.

This will get us a great deal further than merely a typology of all abnormal, average people. Certain insights came from the Lüscher Color Test when it was taken by hundreds of thousands of people in nearly all cultures. We can apply those experiences in a new kind of test, which has the great advantage that you can analyze anyone and everyone and understand people better without their having to be present or even guessing your aim. However, you must know the people so well that you can clearly sense which of the four goal tactics they use and which of the four defense tactics are typical of them. You needn't apply the colors of the color test. Instead, hundreds of signals (clothing, movements, gaze, voice, idioms, interests, home furnishings) will tell you how to categorize them.

I've assembled the eight figures for you like a family photo.

The lower four are the defense tactics. In these cases, as in the color test, the corresponding color is marked with the sign —. The upper four are the goal tactics. The corresponding preferred color is marked with a + as in the color test.*

The Four Goal Tactics (GT)

B the conceited peacock	C the pompous showoff	
A the good-natured angel	Green / Red Blue / + / Yellow	D the expectant dreamer
the knight in armor 4	Yellow / Blue Red / — / Green	the discontented devil 1
	the tormented martyr 3	the agile serpent 2

The Four Defense Tactics (DT)

In a little weather house, when the woman vanishes in one door, the man comes out the other. A defense tactic (—) and a goal tactic (+) depend on each other in the same way. Every — creates a +. And vice versa:

---

*A detailed description of these four basic types and their preferences and behavior can be found in my book *Signals of Personality*.

Every excess (+) is followed by a lack (−). You can never tell ahead of time which defense tactic will lead to which goal tactic. Nor can you predict which goal tactic, for instance bragging, results in which defense tactic, for instance dissatisfaction.

BLUE: UNITY

Blue type:	There is only the one person or thing; hence . . .
Goal tactic:	**The good-natured angel** (+ blue) A
Standpoint:	There's only one thing; hence, I have enough.
Sense of self:	Self-denial
Behavior:	Conformity Compliance Compromise
Goal:	Satisfaction Détente Relaxation Peace without conflict

Do you feel that you're a good person? You are? Then let me tell you about a better one: the good-natured angel. Naturally not an angel with wings. He or she has hands, which do nothing but good.

Do you feel an unspoken admiration when you're in a hospital and a nun comes toward you as a white and holy angel? Or when a nurse crosses your path as a no less white angel? Do you feel you're not such a good person because you admire such an angel but would not like to be one? The good-natured angels are blue types. They live for peace: "Stop fighting! Be nice to each other. It's not all that bad." They bring peace and every kind of satisfaction, for both the soul and the upper body. Not only are the good-natured angels modest ("You can't have everything!"), they have the ambition to be modest ("It's better to give than to receive!"). They are proud of being able to serve, of submitting humbly and denying themselves. They obey out of conviction that it is worthwhile. The good-natured angel, confident of victory, can develop himself or herself in assistance and solicitude. Good-natured angels have a sure instinct for the weak and for the weaknesses of their victims.

But what does a good-natured angel get out of it?

What profit does such a person draw from all the nurturing and self-sacrifice? Good-natured angels expect their victims to enslave themselves in eternal gratitude and devotion. Angels believe they can store up the spoiled and hence dependent children or mate for lonesome hours or for their old age. Good-natured angels regard their love and care as a longterm loan that will someday be paid back by one's children, by the partner accustomed to dependence, or, at the very latest, by heavenly justice. The good-natured angel always adjusts, for the sake of peace. They put their own needs aside ("One just can't be like that!") and make compromise their life attitude. They thereby undermine their normal self-respect. But even here they are talking themselves into something: "It's not all that bad." They leave not only the recompense for their good deeds to God, but also their fate in life ("What will be, will be."). These "heavenly hosts" like to wear the angel's uniform of pastors, monks, nurses, or Salvation Army soldiers. To stress their family intimacy, they address one another as brother and sister.

But they often feign away the need for an intimate physical union. That is why it can often be found as an unsatisfied drive on the back side of the icon. The good-natured angel very often suppresses the dissatisfied devil in himself or herself. They feed their devil with song and prayer. Angels want to convert the devil in themselves. Yet they mostly address everyone but themselves with moralizing and missionizing.

You can recognize good-natured angels in their gestures as well. They tilt their head to the side, bow like bellhops, and crawl toward you all ears. Though they act empathetic, sympathetic, and sensitive toward you, they are often merely passive good listeners.

Their speech tempo is calm, their voice rather mellow. Good-natured angels are often aesthetes; their grooming is careful and more on the traditional side. They absolutely never dress extravagantly. They wear a single color, usually a modest one, and never a gaudy pattern. If they wear jewelry, then it's never excessive or showy. On the other hand, their jewelry is aesthetically exquisite or traditional and is often worn as a souvenir.

The good-natured angel has a calm, veiled gaze, sometimes even the sad, devoted eyes of a St. Bernard dog (incidentally, a canine breed that they especially like next to Newfoundland or cocker spaniel).

If good-natured angels aren't just flaunting their usual amiability, but are really in love, then their great faculty for devotion can develop an unexpectedly powerful erotic intimacy. At this point, the good-natured angel and the dissatisfied devil blend in the fulfilled love of normality.

Defense tactic:	**The dissatisfied devil** (−blue)	1

Standpoint:	There is only the one thing or person, therefore I would like more.

Sense of self:	Dissatisfaction with oneself

Behavior:	Disquiet
	Agitation
	Greed
	A fear of being short-changed

Defense:	Against dissatisfaction
	Against deprivation
	Against bleak emptiness
	Against the vortex of depression
	Against boredom

Men and women who are attractive during the first half-hour, nerve-wracking during the second, and alone again during the third never come out of their hell. Instead they drag in everyone who is defeated in the first round. The fidgety cheerfulness, the hectic fascination, and the enthusiastic openness are a straw fire in the discontented devil. The fire blazes as long as they are not pulled down by the "depressive vortex," as long as they surface from the pit of loneliness.

Their problem is finding a sense of togetherness and solidarity with a partner and feeling at home in a group. Because of an infantile disturbance in their relationship to their mothers, they have never known relaxed closeness. They don't have the solid foundation of trust which can ultimately outlast all sensitivities and conflicts.

This inner isolation can lead to a depressive "emotional illness." Such people will either try to deaden it

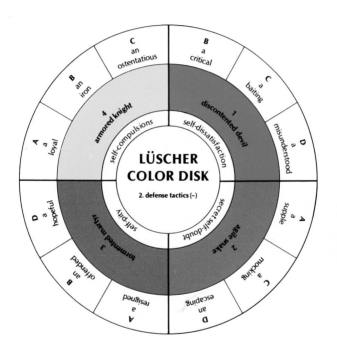

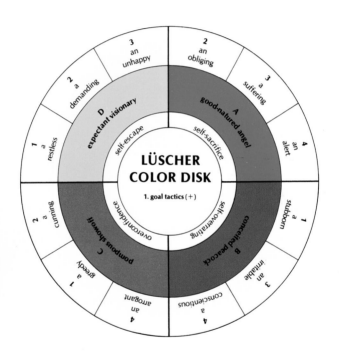

LÜSCHER COLOR DISK

1. goal tactics (+)

A good-natured angel
- 2 an obliging
- 3 a suffering
- 4 an alert
- self-sacrifice

B conceited peacock
- 1 a stubborn
- 3 an irritable
- 4 a conscientious
- self-overrating

C pompous showoff
- 1 a greedy
- 2 a cunning
- 4 an arrogant
- overconfidence

D expectant visionary
- 1 a restless
- 2 a demanding
- 3 an unhappy
- self-escape

with alcohol and tranquilizers or flee the depressive vortex with a hectic hustle and bustle. They are "full of go," which the psychiatrist describes as "agitated." Because of the inner isolation, the dissatisfied devils, incapable of trust and devotion, feel their relations to others as more or less empty. Hence they live with the feeling: "That's too little, I want more." They feel emotionally and thus often sexually undernourished. Whatever is offered them, they find meager and unsatisfying. That's why they're hungry for experience. "Why should I do without? I want to give it a try."

If the condition lasts, as it usually does, then their greed becomes a mania, an addiction. Along with alcohol, smoking offers constant satisfaction. (In my color test, among the 5,300 smokers tested, those who inhaled strong cigarettes frequently rejected blue.)

The discontented devils have only their one mouth as a chimney and cigarette holder and only their one throat as a conduit for alcohol. However, they've got two eyes and a TV set to deaden their urge for more. They've even got a rationale: the six-o'clock news. It not only feeds them with sensations; it serves as an excuse and curtain-raiser for the next something, for anything.

Discontented devils drug themselves with powerful stimuli and promiscuity. Their lack of devotion to their mates prevents fulfillment and satisfaction, causing them to keep looking for new partners. The man becomes a Don Juan, the woman a nymphomaniac.

If a discontented devil asked me for a diagnosis I would say: "Cannot adapt to the given possibilities; incapable of self-moderation; must be certified as a rather discontented devil."

I hope you can empathize with the discontented devils enough to know what you have to reckon with in their case. They feel they never get their fair share because they regard their situation, relationship, or attachment as empty, boring, and too poor in stimuli and variety. They believe they are "frustrated" and must do without things necessary for their inner satisfaction. They are like a volcano, which is forever seething. You can sense that in their sensitivity. The volcano is always hot and unpredictable, which you can tell by their irritability. The volcano can suddenly erupt and explode and hurl mighty boulders. You can feel this on your head.

There's something boiling there—as you can tell by a volcano's eruption or the discontented devil's expression. When they are greatly excited, their eyes become swift pendulums. Their tongue pushes out to the upper lip. Often it whips back and forth there. The impatient devils like to drum their fingers on a table and jiggle their feet under the table. Others whirl a tuft of hair around their forefinger or fiddle with their clothes. The greedy sucking on a cigarette reveals that their agitation comes from a feeling of emptiness. Others suck on the spaces between their teeth in order to provide some activity for their unsatisfied greed.

Figures of speech very clearly betray their inner attitude. Discontented devils are irritable and impatient; they have inwardly detached themselves from their partners and want to run away from them almost daily, and may even have gotten as far as the railroad station. So they decide: "Ah, it's all so meaningless."

The large-scale discontented devils indulge in hysterical scenes and force their mates and relatives, their vases and kitchen pots, into a true Walpurgis Night.

There are hundreds of ways to recognize discontented devils. The way they pile the butter on their bread, or how often they move, change, and add to the furniture and indeed everything that isn't nailed down. If a person changes partners the moment he or she gets on a first-name basis and a pet-name intimacy; if a person is drawn to shoe stores, fashion boutiques, or jewelry counters like a hound to a bitch in heat; if someone buys things merely to deaden his or her dissatisfaction, disillusion, and emptiness—that person must be counted among the discontented devils.

If a discontented devil says yes to the following statements, then tranquilizers and psychiatric sessions are in order:

Lately I've been acting so irritable and irascible.

I always feel so nervous and driven.

I simply don't have the patience to read a book or a long newspaper article.

I don't have the patience really to listen to someone.

Sometimes I feel like smashing something.

Sometimes I'm so confused that I don't know what to do first.

Maybe I'm too impatient.

Even though I'm wiped out at night, I can't sleep.

GREEN: NECESSITY

Green type:	It's necessary, hence . . .
Goal tactic:	**The conceited peacock** (+ green) **B**
Standpoint:	It's necessary for me, hence I absolutely want only this and nothing else.
Sense of self:	Self-overestimation
Behavior:	Authoritarian
	Arrogant
	Ironical
	Dogmatic
	Intolerant

Goal: Self-assurance
                Self-assertion
                Getting your own way

Peacocks don't do anything. They merely stand there, preen their feathers, and spread their tails as though saying, "Look at me, I'm beautiful." That is the essential difference between them and the pompous braggart. The peacock regards himself or herself as wonderful. Braggarts, however, do everything in their power to make that impression on others. The boastful showoff is often a snob and always pompous. The conceited peacock, on the other hand, feels important. In their self-overrating they feel superior, better, part of a special elite. The reasons are ultimately trivial and certainly unconnected with any facts. Peacocks may be proud that their family tree can be traced back to the apes. Or they consider themselves intelligent. A pretty girl easily becomes a conceited peacock if her attractive face gets a lot of attention and she sees that attention as a yardstick for her inner worth and self-respect.

People become conceited peacocks if they merely talk themselves into having self-respect and feel conceited about something unreal: beauty, intelligence, background, property, moral virtue. They actually believe beyond the shadow of a doubt that they are exactly as they imagine themselves to be in their conceit or as a group in society judges them to be.

Like the other three normal senses of self (self-confidence, self-moderation, self-development) which make up a "good conscience," self-respect is not a quality that one can take possession of. A "good conscience" and self-respect exist only as long as I use the guiding norms (ideals) as signposts for my decisions and actions. That is why a venal judge is no longer a judge. This is why the Pharisee, who scorns self-moderation as a guiding norm, is a conceited peacock: "Dear God, I thank you that I am not like them." Such people spread the tail of their virtues. They are self-complacent, which destroys their self-respect. Arrogant pride is an unsuitable self-heightening. Self-respect, which is always merely a guiding norm of action, is replaced by arrogance and self-overrating. The person who judges from an arrogant standpoint is not only immodest, but also not objective, and thus his or her decisions are unreasonable. Ergo: They are stupid. Arrogance is not only the facade of stupidity. It is also the cause of stupidity.

Self-respect comes from acting on your conviction. No external assurance, no self-assurance, no trophies or distinctions, not even the greatest acorns in the oakleaves will promote your self-respect. On the contrary, people who try to build their moral self-respect by proving themselves will merely destroy it. It's like painting a house facade when the foundation is too weak.

Conceited peacocks have many figures of speech that betray them and their authoritarian arrogance. The shortest is "Ha ha!" The most impressive: "Do you know whom you're talking to?"

Far more frequent and common: "How dare you!" A showoff and a snob who's learning how to be a peacock will ruffle his or her feathers with the words "I've got every right in the world" or "They have their nerve!" or "If they imagine that I'm going to. . . ."

Irony is a deportment that some peacocks cultivate to perfection and enjoy to the hilt. The statement of irony is seeming admiration. But it's either so exaggerated or so banal that the person who says such a thing can't possibly be serious. The victim is made to look ridiculous, and peacocks preen their proud feathers.

Most medals are the tin signs of a peacock club. The members of a peacock farm may decorate themselves with Rotarian medals or nose rings. But their goal is always the same: to distinguish themselves as elite birds. When working peacocks have to deal with one another, their mode of address is "Colleague."

The conceited peacock prefers elitist, self-willed breeds of dogs; for example, the basset, the chow chow, the borzoi, or the Afghan. And if the braggart is present at the selection, then the great Dane.

Conceited peacocks spread not only their tails but also their legs, like an officer in boots.

They stick out their chests as though they want to be covered with decorations, and they hollow their backs. Since this often becomes a permanent posture, they have a tendency toward chronic back pain. With their heads lifted high, they like to look down. The top peacocks sit on a high horse, lift their eyebrows, and have mocking smiles and flaring nostrils. The lesser peacocks gaze with blasé aloofness at the far horizon and lift their teacups with their pinkies straight out.

You can see that conceited peacocks are not braggarts showing off their importance. They *feel* important.

The conceited peacock has a schizoid attitude toward sexual attractions and a miserable attitude toward erotic enthusiasm. Sex functions as a release for their inner tension and often as a means of dominating their mates. So their unions don't turn into close intimacy. They remain inwardly aloof. This is expressed openly by a moral putdown or by impotence and frigidity, or by difficulty in reaching orgasm.

The release of sexual tension, on the other hand, is

sought in masturbation or in relations that are ultimately nothing but masturbation by way of the partner.

The inner constraint and the excessive demand that conceited peacocks place on their achievements or on the people around them reach an abnormal pitch if they can say yes to the following statements—in which case psychotherapy would be in order:

I think I'm very conscientious.

The least disorder can drive me bananas.

I'm accustomed to counting unimportant things, like streetlights and windows.

I often memorize unimportant numbers, like license plates.

Sometimes I worry that I've left on a light or the gas or I haven't locked the door; or I haven't stamped, addressed, or sealed a letter; I always have to check and see.

There are certain things I always feel driven to do.

Sometimes I fear I have to do something specific, against my will.

Sometimes I'm helplessly haunted by a thought, a tune, or an idea.

I often have a need to walk over stones or up or down steps in a certain way.

Defense tactic: **The agile serpent** (– green)   2

Standpoint: It's necessary for me, so I want to do not only this but also that absolutely. I don't want to be short-changed.

Sense of self: Secret self-doubts

Behavior: Excessive demands that absolutely have to be met

Don't want to do without, hence necessary diplomacy

Clever, cunning, evasive

Want to free themselves, "emancipate themselves," put off decisions

Defense: Against limiting their needs

Against giving up on their demands

Against obstacles to their free choice

Against dependency

Way back in paradise, the serpent played a seducer's role. It gave blameless Eve the poor reputation of having female character traits. Ever since, we've known not only that Eve can be seduced, but that she uses such unfair devices as ripe apples to seduce men.

The agile snake is the hidden back side of the conceited peacock. The snake also makes his or her demands. Sometimes not big ones, but many. Sometimes big ones *and* many. It began with an apple, as we all have learned. Later, it was a fur coat in order to be independent of the weather. Then it was a second car in order to be independent of the husband. Now it's a lover in order to be even more independent of the husband.

If a woman, the agile snake makes demands that only a gorgeous Adonis can fulfill—if he's got the mind of an Einstein, the heart of an Albert Schweitzer, the artistic originality of a Pablo Picasso, and above all the wallet of a John D. Rockefeller. If a partner doesn't happen to combine all these useful characteristics, then the agile snake finds perfection with partners that complement one another either simultaneously or in succession. The cunning serpent writhes with diplomatic agility past the imperfections of creation and the barriers of society ("Once doesn't count"). Her independence drive used to be called disobedience, then infidelity, and now emancipation. For the sake of emancipation, the agile snake takes all kinds of risks. The right hand must never know whom the left hand is calling ("That's nobody's business"). Agile snakes regard their situation, usually marriage, as forced upon them. They want to break out and be free. So they consider order stodgy, and anyone who doesn't reject order is a philistine. As agile snakes, they never commit themselves and they put off making up their minds, so as to keep all possibilities open and assure themselves of all advantages.

Perhaps the agile snake was spoiled as an only child or youngest child or favored as an only boy or only girl among other children. In any event, it's hard for such a person to put up with limitations, to chew the dry bread of duty, and digest renunciation. If he or she doesn't like doing the dishes, then they are forgotten ("Let it wait"). A female serpent mends a hemline with a safety pin. Likewise the male snake understands how to get out of doing things and avoid unpleasant things. He has no time because he's got to read the paper. Later on, he has no time because there's nothing he hates so much as being forced to do something. And that's also the only thing he is consistent and persevering about. The agile serpent has a knack for interesting others, then fascinating them, in order ultimately to manipulate them. The rabbits who fall for the tactical charm of agile serpents will enjoy their favor as long as what they do will help the serpents slither toward their goal. Cunning serpents are not only attractive on the outside. They are also quick-witted, often appearing more intelligent than they really are. They play their role to perfection, leaving no traces behind—neither lipstick nor a bank account.

The agile snake is the back side of the peacock. As a serpent, he or she has kept a proud peacock heart, but fully transformed the tactic. Both of them, the peacock and the snake, are after a confirmation of their worth. Conceited peacocks overrate themselves. They believe they have an elite worth. They merely need the proper recognition. On the other hand, agile snakes see that they cannot take recognition or the fulfillment of their demands for granted. Things don't just drop into their laps. They even sense that the imagined worth can never be their genuine worth, and hence does not suffice for self-respect. The snake is full of self-doubts. Not only do they have to "crawl on their belly" and "eat the dirt," but their sense of self has a soft spine. They experience their self-doubt briefly as stagefright, but chronically as a feeling of inferiority, and secretly as self-scorn. They adroitly camouflage their insecurity, often their inhibitions, behind a proud manner that frequently strikes others as blasé. However, since agile snakes are actually full of self-doubts, they hunger for reassurance. Like busy little bees, they flit from flower to flower, gathering looks of admiration and compliments.

But they are not bees that bring home honey. They are serpents biting their own tails. No successful show of theirs, no sexual conquest, no clutch for reassurance ever catches what they really need for their self-doubts. They never find the necessary self-respect. Instead of acting in accordance with their ethical norms and convictions and thereby achieving self-respect, they try to drug themselves with prestige-laden self-assurances, from diamond pendants to honorary titles.

This chronic self-assurance, these orgies of ego massages and self-admiration, undermine the self-respect. The increasing self-doubts lead to self-scorn and despair, and thus to moral suicide. Real suicide is often the ultimate, the fatal attempt at finding the necessary self-respect ("I wanted to prove that I wasn't a total failure"). But it's merely one more useless effort at deadening their self-doubt with self-assurance. People who don't know the importance and effectiveness of the senses of self are amazed: "And he was such a gifted young man, too."

In a woman, the serpent's mimicry is seductive. Her eyes shine expectantly, the corners of her finely curving mouth are set at ten of two. But if the awaited reassurance fails to come, then the corners of her mouth sink down to twenty past self-scorn.

The agile serpent often has long, slender hands. When they express her emotions, the fingers or palm seem to catch and ensnare everything or else push it away.

These gestures reiterate the double direction of emancipation: defense and liberation. They express the agile serpent's dilemma between dependency on her demands and her demand for independence.

The fear of confinement, from which the agile snake is striving to escape, is known in psychiatry as claustrophobia. If you can say yes to the following statements, then you will improve with psychiatric consultation and tranquilizers or neuroleptics:

Criticism offends me deeply and discourages me.
I have a hard time making decisions.
I get embarrassed easily.

I have no self-confidence.

Usually, my fear of not succeeding prevents me from trying something new.

I get scared in a dense crowd of people.

I'm scared when I'm alone in a room, especially when it's small and closed.

I'm afraid of certain animals (spiders, mice).

RED: MULTIPLICITY

Red type: There are so many things, therefore . . .

Goal tactic: **The pompous showoff, braggart** C
                 (+ red)

Standpoint: There are so many things, therefore I
                 want more.

Sense of self: Overconfidence

Behavior: Trying to impress others
                 Putting on the dog

Goal: To be thought of as an important and
                 interesting personality

The brave little tailor wrote "seven at one blow" on his chest. He preened himself with truth—the seven were flies—and that was his deception.

If he hadn't made much of himself with the seven, everyone would have asked: Seven what? But with his pompous pose, the brave little tailor made others think he had killed seven giants.

A half-truth, a white lie, contains glib deception.

The man who owns a one-man firm and calls himself a director is not lying. But he's using a half-truth to make himself sound important.

And that's exactly what I mean by a showoff. With false casualness they drop the names of the important people they associate with or are even friendly with. They hint at how influential, how important, how wealthy they themselves are. If they are afraid their boasting will be seen in its true light, then they also name the price they paid, in order to have their figures prove how honest—and lacking in taste—they are.

Showoffs are a red type. Their leitmotif is: There are so many things that impress me; therefore I would like to have a lot more to impress others.

They are pompous. They think they know all the answers. And perhaps even all the questions. They feel like a little tailor who is impressed with what can impress the masses. All they care about is quantity. They have no use for quality. Hence, the important thing for them is whatever is well known, not what is good and genuine.

People who admire something to which they don't authentically relate are members of the widespread kitsch club. It is not the object itself that is kitsch, not the Kewpie doll. It is the inauthentic relationship that a person has to the object or the situation. Neither the Kewpie doll nor the necklace of artificial pearls is kitschy—but rather the person who wants to feign emotions with the doll, or wealth with the cultured pearls, or modesty with understatement. Thus, braggarts are as kitschy as kitsch can be. For they don't care about qualitative perfection, or about the congruence of a goal and the shaping toward it. Their only interest is the effect on the unqualified admirer and the unqualified masses. For their inauthentic attitude, every love relationship, every friendship, every work of art, every visit to a play or concert is primarily motivated by social considerations. They even judge a love relationship not by the degree of closeness and intimacy, but by its market value. They calculate how greatly they are envied for it or how attractive it will sound in their memoirs. The showoff's inauthentic relationship makes kitsch out of a genuine object or work, out of a friendship that the partner is sincere about.

The showoff's heaven is prominence. That's the world he or she wants to enter. Every letter of that magic word embodies their personality. That's the one thing they're true pros at.

"If you've got something, you *are* something." That's their philosophy. Machiavelli recommended the same thing to his prince: "Everyone sees what you appear to be; very few feel what you are."

Showoffs make themselves important with two tactics. The first is the mouth offensive, the second the show offensive.

With the first, they tell you what you're to think of them. With the more elegant second one, they want to offer you conspicuous proof of that. They employ sign language, hundreds of wordless signals, to show you what to think of them.

These showoffs really believe that they're prominent personalities because they have a signet ring on a finger or a moped on the other end, an ocelot fur, a swimming pool on the front lawn, a fancy car in front of the garage, or a Havana cigar in the mouth. The showoff has a car that he or she drives only when no one's looking. Otherwise, it serves as conspicuous consumption.

They furnish their homes with shooting irons and bloodthirsty weapons. A snakeskin hangs on the wall, while the floor sports the skin of a beast that would be cruel and dangerous if it weren't flat.

The true snob tries to dazzle you with genuine period furniture and renowned works of art. The first-class showoff sends tingles up and down your spine—not just with a snakeskin, but also with a Ming Dynasty floor vase or a *genuwine* antique thingamabob.

They subscribe blindly to the best-seller list, and their literary education is sufficient for them to weave titles into a conversation at the next party.

The success-hungry braggart is as well groomed as a master tailor going to church. If the braggart is female, she wears a costly dress in the latest fashion. Tattooed on her frock is the couturier's name to let everyone know what stable the taste came from.

In contrast, the snazzy, classy braggart, male or female, dresses in some cheap fad and drives an expensive sports car.

Their pet expressions, on the other hand, betray the showoffs even when you meet them in a sauna. They include: "Of course, that goes without saying." They often affirm something with highly emotional words (Pet expressions as utterances of emotional attitudes are discussed in my book *Signals of Personality*). Some of these emotional words are: *tremendous, fabulous, fantastic;* or, to show how overwhelmed they are: *weird, wild, crazy.*

They say no with words of indignation, like *horrible, terrible, awful, dizzz-gusting.* Words like *Right?, Huh?, Don't you see?, You dig?* are lassos thrown out for reassurance.

Your eyes and ears have been so sharpened that you can instantly recognize our dear friends the showoffs when they say: "This'll knock them for a loop" or "Wait till they get a load of this." Their overconfidence boils down (or up) to self-admiration: "No one can hold a candle to me" or "Just let someone try and match me."

If showoffs also wiggle peacock feathers, then you can hear from the condescending corners of their mouths: "I can do that with my eyes shut." Or the brave little tailor boasts, "Why, that's child's play."

You'll find red types north and south, east and west. The color red is extremely popular, and so is the role of the pompous showoff.

Defense tactic:	**The tormented martyr (− red)**	3
Standpoint:	There's a lot—therefore it's too much for me.	
Sense of self:	Self-pity	
Behavior:	Listless Self-pitying Tired Exhausted Depressive	
Defense:	Against excitement and having excessive demands made on one Against depressive exhaustion Against disdain	

When showoffs vanish inside the weather house, then out come the tormented martyrs. If you ask them "How are you?" they wail: "What can I tell you?" or "Do you really want to know?" or "As well as can be expected." Even if they feel good and life is a bed of roses without thorns, they merely shrug their shoulders and reply, "I'm all right—under the circumstances." If you anxiously ask them about the circumstances, they patronizingly admit, "I can't complain."

Tormented martyrs swim in self-pity like fish in water. They pity themselves and find themselves admirable in this role. They turn an earthworm into a snake, a cat into a panther, every achievement into an arduous effort, and every joy into a duty. The martyr weeps and wails in order to make an impression—like the braggart. Since they can't show off with anything pleasant, they put everything down as baloney—and rather cheap baloney at that. God's world is not a surprise package for them; it's a bag of woes and worries, which they have to carry and endure. They pity themselves and admire themselves as tragic heroes. Since other people won't give them the compliments they expect and won't admire them, they try to offer a good example by admiring themselves. This kind of self-satisfaction does them good. They enjoy themselves in their role of lament like a child having a good cry.

As a martyr, they celebrate their self-pity in all keys—major and minor:

> Resigned: "Well, I just won't talk about it any more." "It's no use."
> Humble: "I've really done everything I could."
> Tragic: "No one understands me." "Everyone's against me."
> Reproachful: "It's always the same old song."
> Indignant: "I've had it." "I'm fed up."
> Almost matter-of-fact: "I'm annoyed."
> Frank: "It's disgusting." "I just don't feel like it."

Now just what, you may ask, is the difference

between the showoff and the martyr? The showoff's goal is to be admired by others—a road that, as we know, is paved with failure and frustration. Tormented martyrs shorten the trip. They don't wait for the dubious applause of others, they merely clap their hands themselves. Of course, neither showoffs nor even martyrs are totally sure of themselves. Martyrs know they make fools of themselves with self-praise. To make up for it, they smear self-pity—as indirect self-admiration—so thickly on their bread that it looks like honey.

Four-Color People know that sticky self-pity feels like drippy sentimentality. We, in turn, are written off as superficial and unsympathetic by martyrs. That confirms, for them, how pitiful they are—thus proving, in their opinion, what they wanted to prove.

If the sun shines on martyrs' full stomachs and if, despite all their efforts, they find no reason for annoyance or self-pity, then they've got a home remedy to help them out of their misery. A showoff had to fly abroad several times for professional reasons, which made him feel like a responsibility-laden man of the world. When there were no problems or trips in the offing, he boasted as a showoff: "If I had to fly abroad now . . ." And he answered himself as a tormented martyr: ". . . it would make me sick."

Instead of actively deploying their energy and ability, and keeping their self-confidence on the move with achievements, showoffs merely ride along on a horse of the same old color. They are disappointed at not winning a race. In this way, showoffs become martyrs, pitying themselves and ultimately foundering in passivity and depression. Martyrs ask too little of themselves and go to pot: "Everything's spoiled for me." Originally, it was a correctable indolence and phony self-pity: "This is awful. I don't want it." But soon it turns into "I can't" because their self-confidence has crumbled.

The feeling of inability ("I can't go back to my old profession") paralyzes the necessary action. Self-pity is followed by incapacity ("I can't"). The circle closes into depressive paralysis, despondency, hopelessness, and melancholy, with all the other signs of depression, like poor appetite, troubled, fitful sleep, early awakening, frequent weeping, and lack of interest.

The tormented martyr has a harmless twin, whom I would like you to meet: the spineless puppet. This marionette, as we know, can be manipulated by a string.

The supposed free will of many men dangles along straight to where the manipulating female hand points. When female lips pout, female eyes weep, and the female heart aches—that is, plays the martyr—then the marionette doesn't realize he's being pulled on a string. A lot of things can be gotten out of the marionette or the henpecked husband.

Self-pity is a disagreeable vice, for it triggers all kinds of depressive moods.

Metabolic disturbances can also cause depressions. If you say yet to the following statements, then psychiatric treatment and antidepressants are in order:

Recently I've been feeling extremely pessimistic.
I don't feel up to my obligations any more.
For some time now, I haven't been enjoying anything.
It's really an effort pulling myself together for anything.
Generally I feel miserable and very down.
I'm tired of everything.
Life is agonizing.
I wish I were dead.

YELLOW: POSSIBILITY

Yellow type: Everything is possible, therefore . . .

Goal tactic: **The expectant visionary** (+ yellow) D

Standpoint: Everything is possible, therefore I'm
                  going to try everything.

Sense of self: Self-escape
                  Feeling independent and free

Behavior: Flight from problems
                  An urge for the wide open spaces and
                     change
                  Optimism
                  Searching, hunting

Goal: To take advantage of and try all pos-
                  sibilities

"That'll work somehow. That's a sure thing." Such are the typical comments of visionaries.

For them, the little word "if" is no hindrance. With their hopes and wishes, visionaries blow up a balloon and float through the sky—visiting all their castles in the air.

So long as they maintain the altitude of their fantasizing, there'll be no danger of their colliding with reality.

However, the visionary's soaring doesn't necessarily have to take place as a delusion behind the walls of an asylum. There are far more ambulant visionaries who never enter a hospital, because their castles reap them enough money and prestige to make them socially accepted and honored.

Man doesn't live by bread alone, he also needs a philosophy. So visionaries ingratiate themselves with the intellectual infantry as philosophy makers, and they make themselves indispensable. A religious fad lasts a couple of weeks. If it's transcendental, a couple of months. If it's psychoanalytical, a couple of years. If it's political, a couple of decades. If it's national, a whole lifetime. And a religious creed only reaches its full fruition after that.

Charging the highest prices, they fob their little cloud castle off on every defenseless sucker—either as a serious popular ideology or as a political pseudo-ideology, as Madison Avenue psychology or as some other -ology. It's not just a matter of intellectual self-sufficiency and good taste, but also a question of your fate, if you, as a 4-Color Person, use your own ideas as your norms or get stuck in the spiderweb of some religious, political, moralistic, or economic ideology.

Visionaries walk the tightrope of self-deception. They defend themselves against reality with the most effective weapon: the reinterpretation of reality (Hitler: "The German nation has disappointed me."). Ultimately, the escape from reality leads to delusion, paranoia.

The harmless visionaries of everyday life are optimist, wishful thinkers, and tightrope walkers, doing their somersaults in thin air. When they plummet into the net of necessity, their excuse is "If it hadn't been for this or that." It's like a trampoline. They'll do anything to avoid the carpet of reality.

Using the adverb *definitely*, they talk themselves and their listeners into something that they secretly doubt: "Tomorrow, the weather will *definitely* be fine."

Visionaries, like peacocks, make an absolute claim. They believe that anything is possible, and available for them—at least to try it out. They are related to the agile snake, who refuses to forgo anything.

This high demand creates a high inner tension in visionaries. They need instant success and satisfaction; otherwise the tension becomes too much for them. They have a low "frustration tolerance." As a result, they can't really see things through and they avoid confrontations. They flee from genuine reality and thus they can't get their own demands realized. They blame their bad luck on others. Self-escape and self-deception become visionaries' life tactics. Thus, they maintain the exorbitant, illusionary claims of their wishful world by ignoring their failings, their failures, and their inadequacies, and saddling them on other people.

They become the restless, eternal, and often unattached seekers of a mirage paradise.

The hopeful visionary clutches at a straw. Expectant visionaries kindle it as a foxfire. They approach a new task or as yet unknown mate full of enthusiasm. However, erotic fascination and often sexual excitability as well slacken to the extent that the mate becomes a familiar reality for them. Then, at the point when genuine love ought to develop, visionaries lose all their erotic fascination. They ignite their next straw fire and continue as a male or female Don Juan.

Visionaries live with one foot in the past, in "the good old days." They regard their present-day situation and partner relationship as provisional or almost a thing of the past. They have their other foot in the future, in which everything will be better and finer.

In contrast, 4-Color People live in the present. For them, every new day means a new life. Fulfillment in the daily present, the 4-Color Persons's happiness— those are things that visionaries don't experience.

They are not Hans-in-Lucks. They are not bon vivants. They are playboys or playgirls.

If visionaries are young, they say, "When I'm grown up. . . ." If they're grown up, they say, "When I get married. . . ." If they have children, they say, "When the kids are grown up. . . ." At their jobs, they dream: "When I retire. . . ."

"Someday" and "Then I'll . . ." are expressions that betray the expectant visionary. The more often someone chokes down unadmitted doubts with *definitely*, and the more uncertain statements are anchored with emergency formulas such as *sort of* or *somehow* or *virtually*, then the more certain you can be that you're dealing with a visionary. Such a person still hasn't outgrown his or her childhood faith that existing reality can be altered by words.

The visionary usually speaks glibly and quickly. Some even stutter or stammer in their excitement.

They love art and illusions. They need change, wide open spaces, and travel for new illusions.

If the visionary's fantastic ideas reach a psychiatric dimension, then they come out as a mania: "Sometimes my thoughts whiz ahead faster than I can utter them." Or: "I have such great ideas so often, that I can't put them all into words." Or as megalomania: "I have a grand and special mission in this world." Or: "I can read other people's minds."

Manic states have to be treated by a psychiatrist.

Defense tactic:	**The armored knight** (− yellow)	4
Standpoint:	Everything is possible, therefore everything is uncertain for me.	
Sense of self:	Self-constraint Feel they have no inner foothold	

Behavior: Conventional
                     Cautious
                     Distrustful
                     Jealous
                     Obstinate
                     Pedantic
                     A collector

Defense: Against disappointment
                     Against rejection
                     Against loss of prestige
                     Against material loss

When visionaries, those wishful thinkers, incurable romantics, and illusion acrobats, have had to take enough disappointments because of their self-deception, they change the direction of their escape from reality. The flight forward, as a goal tactic of the visionary, becomes a flight backward—the defense tactic, the defensive of the armored knight. Their minds escape into a snail shell and their feelings escape into a knightly armor. Both offer safety and security against disappointments.

Mental snail shells are things like ideological creeds—for instance the belief in the Christ child, with all the Christian paraphernalia. Ideological superstition served as an effective cloak for inquisitions and crusades, which brought mortal agony to millions of people. Similarly, the political creeds which, since then, have used inquisitional tortures and political crusades to murder senselessly millions of people.

The knight's armor has several parts. The headgear is the helmet. It's supposed to protect the knight's thinking organ. From underneath the helmet, knights peer cautiously or distrustfully through the protective visor. Whenever knights are up to something behind their shields, their averted faces and their sidelong glares reveal that they are filled with distrust and that they may drop the visor any minute.

In their relationship to their mates, the same distrust bears the spectacular name of *jealousy*. The part of Othello is a starring role for any knight, faithful or unfaithful.

Armored knights cover the chest with a cuirass. Behind it, they conceal their feelings, especially their fear of not being liked. They're afraid to show that they like someone because they might be spurned. They couldn't stand having their armor dented by any putdown—especially from the opposite sex.

However, they're embarrassed about any putdown. And so they never shed their armor. If a man doesn't have a uniform with gold buttons, he hides inside the "neat suit" of the businessman or a dark-blue blazer. And he feels comfortable only with a tie around his neck. The modern knight has a shiny tin suit of armor. Only it travels on four wheels.

Armor is the closest thing to the knight. This strait-jacket gives knights an illusion of security. They think they would "look different" if they ever took off their armor. So nothing can look different; everything has to look normal and go according to a detailed plan.

Knights want to protect themselves against every kind of loss and be defended against disappointments. They require security at any price. In order to feel secure, they require order, both in back and in front. They need it around them and inside them. They force themselves to be orderly and dutiful and put themselves under constant constraint. The latter becomes an achievement compulsion, a success compulsion, and, above all, a drive for self-assurance. The defensively armed and armored knight needs order and constraint in order to feel safe. "What would people think? What would people say?" That's how many of their bashful sentences begin. Their end should be in all honesty: ". . . if I did and said what I really felt."

Iron knights ride on their principles. For them, everything has to be pedantically "in order." Even the ballpoint pen has to lie in an orderly fashion on the desk next to the trimly sharpened pencil. Similarly, military order must always be rigid. For only a sense of duty and obedience can beat the enemy.

Knights are scared of freedom. They need the compulsion of order in order to feel safe. They put themselves under pressure all the time and always ask too much of themselves: "I absolutely have to." "It's better to make sure." Or: "You never can tell." Therefore, everything has to be "flawless" so that no one can criticize what they've done "to the best of my knowledge and conscience."

The knight is scared not only of the future, but often of vast and/or high spaces as well. Some knights are scared of flying, and many are uncomfortable about entering a restaurant and being exposed to the gazes of others.

Since armored knights believe that property offers security, they increase their property, heaping up—according to their taste—money, houses, jewelry, artworks. Or else they simply gather tidbits, paper clips, antiques, autographs of celebrities, beer coasters, status symbols, and all kinds of mental and material knightly armors. If the following statements elicit a yes, then the defensive behavior and distrust have reached a limit that calls for treatment.

It is safer not to trust anyone.
Someone hates me.
I think I'm being spied upon.
I think there's a conspiracy against me.

I'm fighting for a just cause even if everyone's against
  me.
Sometimes I feel I'm being persecuted.

TYPE = TYPICAL BEHAVIOR PATTERN

While looking at this family portrait, with its eight
types, did you recognize any of your friends or your
enemies or possibly even yourself in one of the types?

If you answer restrictively, "Yes, in part," then I'll
agree with you. If you also feel that the innocent victim
on whom you focus your gaze has parts of one or the
other type, then I'll agree with you fully.

I hope you won't accuse me of forcing human beings, with their immense wealth of possibilities, into
typological pigeonholes. That would be a misunderstanding.

In Part Four of this book, on functional psychology,
you will see that it is not a matter of sorting all the
people in the world into different pigeonholes—as is
typical of so many typologies.

With the concept of *type,* I do not mean the whole of
man's being. I simply mean nothing more or less than
the behavior pattern that a person prefers in specific
situations—that is to say, *typical behavior.* By *type,* in
contrast to other typologies, I am describing merely
the *typical* patterns, the *typical* functions which, by
definition, anybody would be capable of. Thus, for
instance, we can say that it's typical of certain people
to clear their throats when they are unsure of themselves, or that they are silent when they are unsure of
themselves, or that they constantly laugh when they
are unsure of themselves.

Whether they're in a familiar or new situation, 4-
Color People try to behave suitably—that is, normally,
and not in some way that is typical for them.

In contrast, the average person applies a specific, typical defense tactic in undesirable situations (devil 1, serpent 2, martyr 3, or knight 4). Such people also apply a specific goal tactic that's typical for them, because they think that this is how they'll achieve a desirable situation (angel A, peacock B, showoff C, or visionary D). Thus, people must, at the very least, be described in terms of their favorite goal tactic and favorite defense tactic. We do so with the combination types (subtypes). For instance, we combine the defense tactic of the discontented devil 1 with the goal tactic of the pompous showoff C. The results are, on the one hand, the greedy showoff C1, and, on the other hand, the baiting devil 1C—depending on whether we start with the goal tactic of the showoff C or the defense tactic of the devil 1.

These facts are also the basis of the Lüscher Color Disk, which appears between pages 128 and 129 and can be cut from the book to be put to use.

THE LÜSCHER COLOR DISK

Like the types described above, the color disk has two sides. One side contains the goal tactics. It shows four main types:

A good-natured angel
B conceited peacock
C pompous showoff
D expectant visionary

There are also three subtypes for each type, making a grand total of twelve different goal tactics.

The other side of the disk shows the twelve defense tactics. Which means the four main types:

1   discontented devil
2   agile serpent
3   tormented martyr
4   armored knight

and the three subtypes for each type.

For each main type, the appropriate sense of self is indicated within the inside circle of the disk. This sense of self is the inner motive for the behavior described by the designation of the main type.

For instance, self-pity is in field 3. "Things are rotten. What a pitiful person I am"—the inner motive for the behavior as a tormented martyr, for the wailing, the listlessness, the fatigue, exhaustion, and depression.

Instructions for using the Lüscher Color Disk

Before using the Lüscher Color Disk for the first time, you ought to read the tables in the earlier section, "The Typology of the Non-4-Color Person," to understand the color types and the outer main fields A, B, C, D and 1, 2, 3, 4.

1. Think of a person you know well, whose character you know from observation and experience. However, it shouldn't be someone who is a normal 4-Color Person and lives in equilibrium, because that individual won't be conspicuous by any typical peculiarity.

2. Take the Lüscher Color Disk. Read the four color types in the inside main fields, A, B, C, and D. Decide which color type most accurately refers to this person and note the corresponding letter (for example, A).

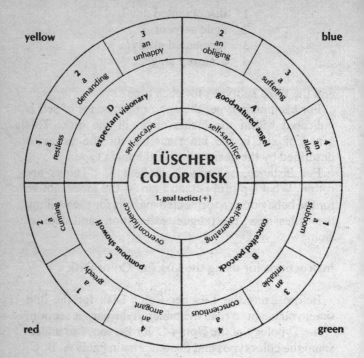

3. Above the main field, there are three fields describing the three subtypes. Try to decide which of the three subtypes comes closest to your friend. To confirm whether your verdict is right, you can check the meaning of this subtype under the corresponding letter and the corresponding number in the tables of this book.

4. Note the number and the letter (3A).

5. On the back of the color disk you'll find (under 3 and A) the back side of that person's character.

6. Check the exact meaning of this subtype in the table

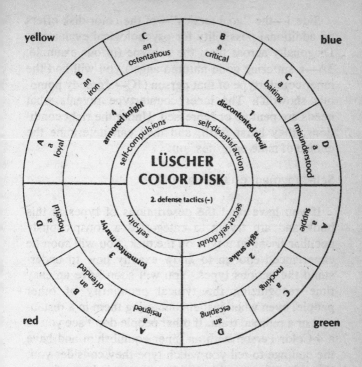

yellow

blue

red

green

C
an
Ostentatious

B
an
iron

A
a
loyal

D
a
hopeful

B
an
offended

A
a
resigned

4
armored knight

self-compulsions

LÜSCHER
COLOR DISK

2. defense tactics (–)

self-pity

3
tormented martyr

B
a
critical

C
a
baiting

D
a
misunderstood

A
a
supple

C
a
mocking

D
an
escaping

1
discontented devil

self-dissatisfaction

secret self-doubt

2
agile snake

(by 3A and A3). Be careful: If the subtype on the back side doesn't fit the person precisely, then you still haven't found the correct and accurate type. So keep looking for the right main type and subtype on the back side of the color disk until the corresponding subtype on the other side of the color disk is accurate.

7. The subtype can also be found by selecting only from among the four main types on the front side and the four main types on the back side. They will give you the letter and the number for the subtype on the front and the back side.

Side 1—the "goal tactics"—of the color disk offers an additional possibility for psychological evaluation. Diagonally across from the subtype (in our example, 3A—a suffering good-natured angel) you will find the inner countertype of that person (1C—a greedy pompous showoff). The inner countertype reveals what needs are pent up or repressed. Under the right conditions, they burst forth, and they can determine the choice of mate or profession.

Self-Judgment on the Color Disk

If you have read the descriptions of types in this book and are trying to categorize a conspicuously peculiar friend in a type on the disk, you will soon be experienced enough to know exactly how to understand the various types. You will soon have an easy time recognizing the typical peculiarity of other people, even when just encountering them in a restaurant or a railroad train. If other people don't see you as a 4-Color Person with an inner equilibrium and have the courage to tell you which type they consider you, then I hope you will experience the great hour of your self-knowledge. You yourself, however, will scarcely succeed in judging yourself as others see you and finding your type plainly on the Color Disk. You won't be able to do it even if others easily and perhaps very clearly see you as one of these types.

THE COMBINATION TYPES

The good-natured angel (p. 93)   **A1**

> In internal conflict with their discontented devil
> Self-sacrifice and self-dissatisfaction

The discontented devil (p. 96)   **1A**

> In internal conflict with their good-natured angel
> Self-dissatisfaction and self-abandonment

The obliging angel   **A2**

Sense of self: Self-sacrifice because of secret self-doubts

Behavior: Adjustment and willingness to compromise in order to avoid disadvantages and to get their way diplomatically, tactically

Obliging angels are conciliatory, smiling, adaptable companions as long as you roll out a soft carpet for them to accompany you on. Their demands are there, but they don't have the courage to voice them, and so they put them aside.

Their tactic is compromise. Peace at any price is more important for them than victory on a heap of shards. They seek a *modus vivendi,* an arrangement with their partners, so that they can get along, or at least get by without colliding. The obliging angel acts friendly so as to avoid conflicts, arguments, fights.

They thereby take on disadvantages and renunciations which, however, cause an inner tension. To get rid of this tension, they try all the harder to prevent conflicts and establish a peaceful harmony.

They are therefore ready to muster sympathy and be loving to their mates so long as they feel that the necessary prerequisites for togetherness are present. Otherwise, they become "critical and obstinate devils."

The agile serpent   2A

Sense of self: Secret self-doubts

Behavior: Supple charm
                    Diplomatic adaptation
                    Clever tactics

Agile serpents want to get their wishes, needs, and way. But they doubt whether they can succeed, for they see the resistance and difficulties. They know that a head-on attack will not help them reach their goal and that their own defenses and perseverance are not sufficient for them to stand their ground and have their way.

Hence, they avoid any direct confrontation, they use adjustment and compromise gradually to reach, or at least get as close as possible to, their goal. Clever tacticians, refusing to play away their trumps, agile serpents never issue an ultimatum. They put off final decisions as long as they can. They never force a choice; they're quite open to alternatives. This tactic gets them much further, even though they have to wait for the right moment. They approach their target step by step, striving for a relationship that is harmonious and as unmarred as possible by conflicts and tensions.

The suffering angel

Sense of self: Self-pity; self-sacrifice

Behavior: Sentimental commiseration
Feels overtaxed
Defense against excitement
Rapidly exhausted; require looking after and consideration
Drug themselves with alcohol, tobacco, compulsive eating, sleeping pills, or piety

Suffering angels act good-natured because they feel compassion and commiseration for themselves and for anyone not as well off as they wish to be. They suffer from their lack of success in regard to their goals, demands, and expectations, and thus they tend to be depressive. They feel weakened and can't believe that they will reach their goals by their own strength.

"It's not going to work. It's all so meaningless." This resignation has gotten the upper hand in them, making them conciliatory on the outside. They have resigned themselves to living with compromises. Their attitude seems tolerant, but actually springs from their helplessness, weakness, inferiority, and resignation.

To avoid wearing themselves out in conflicts, suffering angels often go so far as to give up their true claims. For the sake of external peace, they make concessions that reach the point of self-denial and self-sacrifice.

Suffering angels deaden their conflicts with both compromises and tranquilizers, which is why they need drugs like alcohol or sleeping pills; or else they chain-smoke, eat too much, or numb themselves with piety.

The resigned martyr   3A

Sense of self: Self-pity
                    Sense of inferiority
                    Resigned self-sacrifice

Behavior: Feels overtaxed
                    Fatigue
                    Pessimism
                    Depressions
                    Few interests
                    Little appetite

Resigned martyrs have scrapped their hopes for success and their *joie de vivre*. The world has grown somber for them. They are tortured by their failure to achieve their goals and the desirable situation, and the torment wears them out. It makes them tired and weak. The horizon of their interests keeps shrinking. They become more and more listless. They have no appetite for anything. Their depressive state, the suction toward the depths, casts its shadows on their everyday life and the future. Ultimately, they've had enough of everything, and they wish they were dead.

People get into the state of the resigned martyr because of an unhappy love or the loss of a beloved person or serious professional failures.

Even people who believe they have missed out on a lot, and who refuse to accept the loss of youth because of their hunger for experience, torture themselves over the often merely imaginary barriers of their age. Salient thresholds of age—forty, fifty, sixty—usually cause depressions in the resigned martyr, and they wear on for a long time as *climacteric depressions*.

The alert angel   A4

Sense of self: Self-denial and self-control or
                    self-constraint

Behavior: Loving attentiveness
                    Emotional concentration
                    Need for safety and harmony
                    Urge for security
                    Clinging to an idealized relationship

Alert angels have a strong need for safety and security. They feel comfortable only with a close, emotional tie between them and their love mates as well as
all friends and relatives. They are emotional and
friendly. They like to do things for others. Their joy
and gratitude confirm the feeling of attachment and
security in a close, intimate group. Since alert angels
need a feeling of safety and security, they are atten-
tive, solicitous, and maternal. Since they need safety
and security themselves, they make sure that the solid
attachment is not impaired or shaken by change or any
disturbing influences. Alert angels cling to their mates
and to the relationship because they have not found
any foothold or security in themselves. In solitude,
they feel lost. They are afraid of losing their inner and
outer footholds. The fear of losing any relationship
dominates them and forces them to yield to the point of
self-denial when the relationship is threatened.

Altered, new situations make them insecure and
irritate them so much that they either ignore them as
long as possible or else resist them as long as possible.

The loyal knight   4A

Sense of self: Self-constraint
                    Self-denial

Behavior: Fear of rejection
                     Loyal reliability
                     Honesty
                     Loyalty
                     Patience
                     Conventionality

Loyal knights have their fixed ideal, their idol, and they wish to act accordingly. They are willing to make great sacrifices and renunciations for their great love, their calling and their mission, which strike them as ideals. Secretly, however, they don't feel secure because they have no sufficiently solid foothold inside themselves.

Hence, they need idols, goals, which they idealize and overrate. They want to sacrifice themselves for their idols. They want to dissolve into this idealized love or task, finding the meaning and fulfillment of their life therein. With caution and patience, with constant sympathy and enthusiasm, they devote themselves to their favorite theme, task, and partner. Loyal knights do not discontentedly look around for better possibilities. They limit themselves to the framework of the familiar. Fundamental changes make them insecure, depriving them of what they need most: the feeling of safety, security, and affection.

The stubborn peacock   B1

Sense of self: Discontented
                     Conceited
                     Self-overrating

Behavior: Overbearing
                     Domineering
                     Stubborn

Authoritarian
Intolerant
Impatient
Arrogant

Stubborn peacocks are difficult people. Their inner pride and their vanity make them overbearing, and if something doesn't suit them to a T, they give curt or offensive answers.

They consider themselves an ultimate authority even in areas where they're not one. They not only want to master but also dominate their area. Impatient and irascible, often brusque and defiant, they defend themselves when they feel or imagine that someone is interfering in their territory or questioning their authority or competence.

Stubborn peacocks defend themselves against any dependency—especially when they feel an emotional attachment. They then fear tying themselves inwardly, becoming dependent, and losing their own will and their overbearing claim to superiority. That's why stubborn peacocks conceal their discontent behind a proud, often defiant claim to independence.

They are too embarrassed to admit their yearning for peaceful harmony and a tender and affectionate togetherness. Their pride won't put up with it. To be exact, stubborn peacocks are not pedants, but perfectionists, for their ultimate interest is to reach the perfection and completion of their goals, which fit in with their ideas.

The critical devil   **1B**

Sense of self: Dissatisfaction
                    Self-overrating

Behavior: Irritable
                     Arrogant
                     Reproachful
                     Intolerant
                     Defiant

Of all the discontented devils, the critical devil has the most perfidious tactic for putting through authoritarian demands. These devils know how to dominate or even humiliate others in order to relish their feeling of superiority. Secretly, they suffer from the fact that their dreamed-of harmonious attachment has not come true. They miss the feeling of relaxed intimacy and togetherness. Instead of letting the relationship grow with sympathy and patience, they blame the partner or the situation for lacking the prerequisites.

Critical devils expect other people not only to adjust sympathetically, but also to guess every one of their wishes, thoughts, and expected attentions.

Critical devils are easily irritated and quick to take offense. They not only blame others, but refuse to realize that their own over-demanding expectations trigger the conflicts.

In differences of opinion, they insist on their own standpoint. They refuse to make any concessions, and they turn away abruptly if the other person doesn't come around to their way of thinking.

Many critical and defiant devils try to ignore others or cut them down to size with icy silence. They apply the tactic of withholding love in order to dominate a mate. With this behavior, defiant devils also impair their erotic relationship.

The conceited peacock (p. 99)   B2

In an inner conflict with his or her agile serpent
Self-overrating and secret self-doubts

The agile serpent (p. 103)   **2B**

> In an inner conflict with his or her conceited peacock
> Secret self-doubts and self-overrating

The irritable peacock   **B3**

Sense of self: Self-overrating
            Self-pity

Behavior: Oversensitive
        Irritable
        Quick to take offense
        Easily hurt
        Sulky
        Indignant at unreasonable requests

Irritable peacocks stumble over their self-overrating. Anyone who doesn't justify the peacocks' self-admiration with the proper confirmations will offend them and make them venomous enemies.

For some reason, which is often not even their own accomplishment, irritable peacocks imagine that they are special birds to admire and that people ought to honor their elite uniqueness with respectful attention and consideration. Anyone who doesn't express or at least hint at this special attention is written off by the peacock as being one of the simpleminded common folk, a second-class person of inferior upbringing and education. Depending on their own standpoint, the irritable peacock disqualifies that person as either a philistine or a snob.

In reality, irritable peacocks are offended because their self-admiration is not confirmed. They therefore feel misunderstood and slide into self-pity. Since they secretly doubt whether their self-overrating is congruent with reality, their feelings are hurt by any supposed rejection. They therefore carry on like vain prima donnas, are hypersensitive, and whine and pester people into excusing themselves when they fear that those persons have not respected them as the number-one peacocks in the territory.

The offended martyr   3B

Sense of self: Self-pity
                    Offended pride

Behavior: Feel misunderstood
                    Feel cheated
                    Repugnance
                    Opposition
                    Argumentative

Offended martyrs are wounded in their pride and thus become argumentative rebels. They feel they are fighting for a just cause if, in their feeling of humiliation, they act in protest or opposition, or even just become argumentative.

They are insulted because they feel misunderstood, ignored, and cheated. They find that people have been unfair, insincere, unjust to them. It is humiliating to have people treat them so inconsiderately and unlovingly. They are not only injured, but self-pitying.

The fact that someone underestimates them or treats them like fools hurts their feelings. So they show others whom they are dealing with, "You won't get away with that." They settle accounts, and the settlement can be a matter-of-fact protest or a personal revenge.

The protest easily grows into opposition, or the

opposition is raised to a principle. The irritable peacock becomes an offended martyr, a grouch, a querulant.

The conscientious peacock   B4

Sense of self: Self-overrating; self-compulsion

Behavior: Conscientiousness
Demand for prestige
Claim to expertise
Pedantry
Dogmatism
Compulsion
Caution
Jealousy
Fear of loss
A collector

The conscientious peacock has a quiet but relentless demand for prestige. He or she gets a territory and turns it into a private castle.

Their prestige claims seems, on the outside, like perfectionism. But the internal motive is the power claim of pedantry. With their competence, expertise, or claim to order, they try to create a feeling of security and superiority for themselves and to dominate all others who might make them feel uncertain. Conscientious peacocks don't just know a field or two, they feel competent in all fields. For with this feeling of superiority, they strive to master their secret insecurity, their secret feeling of being lost. They become aware of these feelings mostly as a fear of losing prestige or property. Since they have to fight against their secret insecurity by mastering, ordering, and doing their duty to the point of pedantry, they will brook no symptoms of insecurity. They wave off criticism and reject what they regard as influence.

By a logical, severe, and detailed examination, they try to prove that they are a decisive authority, thereby giving themselves a feeling of solidity and security.

The iron knight   4B

Sense of self:	Self-constraint
	Self-overrating
Behavior:	Zeal
	Industry
	Reliability
	Performance of duties
	Persistence
	Fussiness
	Inflexibility
	Principled
	Sly naiveté
	Fearlessness

Iron knights are afraid they will be disappointed in their expectations and be deluded by illusionary hopes. They are scared of losing their foothold and the solid ground underneath if they give in to uncontrolled wishful thinking and pleasurable fantasies.

That is the secret fear inducing iron knights to force themselves into the iron armor of self-compulsion, fulfillment of duties, industry, and dogged persistence. Iron knights want to prove themselves so that others can count on them. Hence if anything is entrusted to them, they examine and verify it down to the last detail. If the result checks out, it helps their self-assurance. They reckon and calculate in practical and useful terms because anything that is rationally understood and arranged gives them a feeling of security and sets their mind at ease. They distrust all other areas of life, spontaneous vitality and carefree *joie de vivre*. For them, these are illusionary adventures, which they absolutely avoid. They regard them not only as dangerous, but also as irresponsible or immoral. Hence they live according to reformist rules of health, and they try to force their views of life on other people. They are not only didactic, they also want zealously to keep educating themselves. Caution and calculated utility are the alloy from which their knightly armor is forged.

"No pains, no gains" is the bleak motto of their striving for security and recognition.

The greedy showoff C1

Sense of self:	Overconfidence
	Self-dissatisfaction
Behavior:	Tries to impress others, especially by conspicuously acting like an important personality

Of all showoffs, greedy showoffs are among the most ubiquitous and most dissatisfied. Their restless discontent in regard to an achievement and to the existing situation drives them toward a new goal, which is meant to satisfy their hunger for experience and success.

If they are naive enough, they promptly tell everyone they meet all they know and all they have, while dropping names by the bushel, hinting at how influential they are. They not only regard themselves as versatile, wonderful, attractive, and irresistibly sexy, but they also believe that they're as fast as a rocket leaving its ramp. They lack the patience and willingness to adjust lovingly and sympathetically to a given situation. They lack inner modesty. They feel no gratitude for the love they receive, and they remain dissatisfied. This makes the greedy showoff a discontented glutton. They pile up one experience of sex or success after another, the way a jungle tribesman threads his beads. They often flaunt whatever they have to show, like their physique, or a success they've had, or an artwork that they own. The thing they like to do best is to warble their career aria, like an actor or junior executive.

Whether it's auto brands or antiques, successes or travel experiences, wine labels or sexual conquests, greedy showoffs push their trophies in everyone's face until they believe that everyone believes them.

The baiting devil

1C

Sense of self: Dissatisfaction
                  Pompous overconfidence

Behavior: Disquiet
                  Agitation
                  Provoke people in order to create contacts and relationships and to ward off their void (a life which is devoid of relationships), their boredom, their deserted isolation, and their discontent

Baiting devils are dissatisfied because, although highly excitable and emotionally susceptible, they suffer from their lack of responsiveness, their monotony, and their lack of relationships with others. They feel fine if there is an intense encounter and erotic fascination in a relationship. And they like tasks in which they have to commit themselves personally and totally.

Baiting devils can't stand people who hide their true feelings behind conventional clichés and, in their boredom, create a gap and a vacuum. So they bait such people. They challenge them with directness or boorish criticism. They try to strike them in their weak points. That makes the baiting devils feel superior, thereby avenging themselves for the inadequate, unsatisfying attempt at contact or for an earlier rejection.

The shrewd showoff   C2

Sense of self: Pompous overconfidence due to secret self-doubts

Behavior: Uses external devices and a pose of superiority to impress others as an important and interesting personality
Needs constant reassurance

Shrewd showoffs live for the facade they construct between themselves and others in order to impress them. The motive of their actions is the reassurance and admiration they need from others. They hide their self-doubts behind their flaunting behavior—often so well that they don't perceive them themselves, at least as long as they adroitly and quick-wittedly do their superiority act for their audience.

With hackneyed original expressions or with newly packaged standard jokes, with secret tips on food or sex or investment opportunities, with low-voltage relationships that they transform into high-voltage transmissions, they make themselves supermen or superwomen.

Shrewd showoffs want to prove to others—in reality to themselves—that they're smart, superior, admirable. Earning an honest living like other people does not prove any superiority. So they want to shine as clever businessmen or businesswomen, or else they dream about an ingenious coup that would bring them instant fame and fortune.

Not only do they dream about the super coup they're going to pull off—they also talk about it. But, not seldom, they say they can't talk about it: for one thing, they want to attract attention, and for another, they don't want to look like fools if once again nothing comes of it.

The shrewd showoff leads people astray, like the Pied Piper of Hamelin, if they're still as gullible as children—and they believe his or her fairy tales, tall stories, and advertising slogans.

The mocking serpent   2C

Sense of self: Secret self-scorn and self-doubts

Behavior: Aggression for self-assurance
                     Flippant reproaches for self-defense
                        and self-justification
                     Impulsive comments and wounding
                        humiliations

Mocking serpents know how to use a quick, sharp tongue against anyone who gets in their way. Their humiliation venom injures and paralyzes. Fast as lightning, they whiz to the fighting line to battle against any restriction of their interests, any reproach, any pressure. Their aggression either justifies or defends their rights and freedom.

Secretly, they doubt themselves and their ability to make good their claim to freedom. Therefore, they feel harassed by the demands made on them. They are uncertain whether they can meet those great demands, and they don't want to commit themselves with any constraining attachments. If they are enthusiastic about doing something, then they'll do it with élan and tactical skill. If they are put under external pressure or compulsion, then they'll refuse to do it. If they feel hit in their secret self-doubt, then they'll swiftly counterattack.

Whenever the demanded measure of recognition doesn't come, then their ironical arrogance becomes a permanent stance. They need a victim whom they can humiliate with words and deeds in order to relish their superiority. Their arrogance conceals their secret self-contempt from others and from themselves.

The pompous showoff (p. 108) **C3**

   In inner conflict with his or her tormented martyr
   Overconfidence and self-pity

The tormented martyr (p. 112) **3C**

   In inner conflict with his or her pompous showoff
   Self-pity and overconfidence

The arrogant showoff **C4**

Sense of self: Overconfidence

Behavior: Zeal

Requires experiences of success
Strives for reassurance
Wants to play an impressive part
Arrogant claim to admiration
Vanity
Pretentiousness

Arrogant showoffs are vain. In secret, they're anxious about whether they can get all the admiration and recognition that they expect from others.

They want to play an impressive part and constantly need to be reassured as to how good, how great, how wonderful they are. Praise and admiration from others are success experiences they need the way an actor needs applause.

To keep obtaining this admiration, they put in a lot of time and spend even more money. They like everything that feeds the ego. So, they make a great point of dressing attractively. They go into hock in order to stuff their clothes closet and fit themselves out splendidly. Since they want very special things, they have to shell out. Things that other people consider luxuries are just right and proper for the arrogant showoffs.

They decorate themselves with things that are expensive and hence loved by snobs. Since they constantly want to make an impression, every encounter becomes a contest. They compete with all and sundry for a social and professional position. They always compare: their income, their property, their sex appeal, their intellectual superiority, their physique, their athletic performance, the speed at which they can drive their car from one town to another, the amount of liquor they can hold, the speed with which they get well and out of a hospital.

Arrogant showoffs are inwardly dependent on admiration, which they demand with their gradiose lifestyle. They eye the other person with suspicion, to see to what extent they can impress that person. And there's nothing they can endure less than personal criticism. Anyone who doesn't admire them with gaping eyes, anyone who doesn't marvel at their braggadocio and jet-set act, will be waved off as boring, stricken from their party lists, and expelled from their kitsch paradise.

The ostentatious knight   **4C**

Sense of self: Self-constraint

Behavior: Ambition
                   Requires success experiences and
                       reassurance
                   Arrogant attention-getting
                   Jealousy for fear of losing love
                   Competition mania
                   Envy for fear of reduced prestige

Ostentatious knights hide behind gilded armor. Anything regarding them or connected with them has to shine. Other people's admiration gives ostentatious knights a feeling of security. They need reassurance, recognition of their personal achievements. This makes them ambitious.

They push themselves and demand accomplishments of themselves that lead to success and will make them attractive. As an ostentatious, pompous knight, they set great store by their prestige with others and society. They decorate themselves and their territory with prestige signals. They accept only people who pay them respect and admiration. They have little sympathy for other people's opinions. This makes them intolerant and jealous, for they are afraid of losing prestige. For all their distinguished pomposity, they are inwardly unfree, fear all criticism, and are afraid of making fools of themselves.

They follow their success goal with driving intensity and persistence.

They zealously and ambitiously follow their life goal of increasing their social prestige.

The restless visionary

D1

Sense of self:	Dissatisfied
	Self-escape
Behavior:	Restless seeking
	Fickle, agitated
	Separation
	Flight from depressive states

Restless visionaries are eternal seekers. They still haven't found the thing(s) that can offer them fulfillment, happiness, and satisfaction. They flee the present and reality because they can't find the understanding and sympathy that make them feel close and intimate. They regard the unsatisfying situation as bleakness and dullness, and so they flee it. They look for new stimuli and focus expectantly on any new thing that surfaces as a possible experience.

They are afraid of being hurt, which prevents them from courageously and trustingly telling a mate how they feel. They thereby create an alienating vacuum. Since this situation leaves them dissatisfied, they are unable to relax, to find peace and quiet, satisfaction, or harmonious fulfillment. They run away so as not to suffer any more from their dissatisfying void. Their restless seeking comes from a drive to flee the sorrowful vacuum and inner emptiness. They are filled with the hope of finding a mate and a life situation that will bring them peace, harmony, and satisfying fulfillment.

The misunderstood devil

1D

Sense of self: Self-dissatisfaction

Behavior: Restless seeking
Escape from an unsatisfying situation
Lack of security, intimacy, or closeness
Agitated depression

Misunderstood devils are not rooted in any emotional relationship. They lack the security of intimate closeness. Dissatisfied with their situation, they "don't feel at home" in it, and thus they find no peace and relaxation and no fulfillment. They expect more understanding from others, more sympathy, and a greater harmonious rapport. They turn away inwardly from this unsatisfying situation, close themselves off, are irritable, impatient, and focus their feelings on new hopes and expectations. The restless search for new possibilities and better conditions and for an ideal, fulfilling rapport makes them fickle, driven, makes them want to run away. Instead of patience, understanding, and cooperative contentment, there is more and more impatience, irritability, and quick disappointment.

The secret suspicion that their hopes and expectations will continue to be dashed gives the misunderstood devil a basic mood of agitation and depression. This condition lasts as long as they are unwilling to show tolerance and sympathy as well as loving closeness.

The demanding visionary   # D2

Sense of self: Self-escape

Behavior: Excessive, illusionary expectations
                     Refuses to forgo any advantages
                     Exorbitant, fastidious demands
                     Relentless emancipation

Demanding visionaries refuse to do without anything they like. For them, freedom and independence
mean demanding, and availing themselves of, anything
that strikes them as interesting, as an attractive new
experience. They want it so that they can glean the
pickings any time. That's why they arrange and manipulate their obligations until they no longer perceive
them as an unreasonable constraint.

They are demanding and seemingly picky. In reality,
however, they always pick whatever distinguishes
them, is useful to them, and therefore strikes them as
advantageous. Demanding visionaries live in the notion that they have to escape the existing circumstance
since it hinders the development of their potentials.
Any life situation in which all possibilities are not open
to them strikes them as confining and unreasonably
constraining. They regard themselves as emancipated,
thereby justifying their freaky actions. They regard
themselves as original even though they lack authenticity and the capacity for deep, emotional relationships.

Change, the fascination of the new, the expansion of
their horizon, the unusual, the reform, the centrifugal
widening of their territory become the life content of
the demanding visionary. They scorn conservative
order as philistine narrowness and try to escape it with
their fantastical activities.

The demanding visionary lays claim to anything he or she considers possible. That is why they put off making up their mind and live makeshift lives.

The escaping serpent   2D

Sense of self: Secret self-doubts or self-scorn and self-escape

Behavior: Exorbitantly demanding
                   Refuses to forgo anything, hence: agilely diplomatic, clever, refined, evasive, secretive, finds excuses, puts off decisions, in order to keep all advantages open
                   Arranges things for own benefit

Faithless, escaping serpents are always fleeing themselves. They make exorbitant demands, but not so much on themselves as on others. That's why what they have and what's offered to them are not enough. They have to have whatever they find interesting and engaging. Fearing that their claims could be rejected, they wriggle toward their goal along secret paths. Arguments and cogent excuses come to them so quickly that other people believe those explanations and doubt even what they've seen with their own eyes. These serpents wipe away clues, organize and manipulate conditions for their own benefit in order to keep as free of obligations as possible. Escaping serpents hunt for fascination. They always have a new goal and they want to reach it quickly and directly. They have little patience and less persistence.

They are fleeing from themselves and hence fleeing forward. They need wide open spaces and feel fine when flying through the air.

Such a woman's thoughts serve her escape and her feelings serve flirtation. She acts like a pretty and spoiled only child. She arranges her obligations in such a way that she can be as unburdened as possible and devote herself to her greed for experience, as free and as carefree as possible.

The unhappy visionary D3

Sense of self: Self-escape due to self-pity

Behavior: See themselves as being in a difficult, contrary situation and therefore feel self-pity

Unhappy visionaries feel that they are in a transitional situation. They hope that the present, contrary circumstances will somehow change so that they can overcome the burdening problems. They regard their present difficulties as unjust and in no way their fault. Unhappy visionaries feel sorry for themselves and can get entangled in torturous brooding. This wears them out. They are soon exhausted and require careful treatment and consideration.

They lack a realistic, reasonable viewpoint, self-assured decisiveness, and the determination to fundamentally change their conditions in the not-too-distant future.

So they daydream all the more and live in the hope of new, liberating, and carefree conditions, which will help them toward a better life situation.

The hopeful martyr 3D

Sense of self: Self-flight due to self-pity

Behavior: Afflicted by tormenting disappoint-
                        ments
                     Unhappy
                     Regards demands as unreasonable
                        and unendurable
                     Wishful thinking
                     Flight from problems
                     Optimistic illusions

Hopeful martyrs would be the unhappiest people under the sun if they weren't in a frying pan. They are happy only when switching from the frying pan to the fire.

Of course, they're not at all satisfied with their situation. They think they can't stand it, but they do stand it. Other people, who are more decisive and self-confident, are amazed at the hopeful martyrs' involuntary forbearance: Destiny lies on them like an evil spell that they seemingly cannot shake off. Destiny appears to have nailed them to the cross of their illusions. Here, in their fanatic wishful thinking, lies the self-deception to which the hopeful martyr falls prey. They sacrifice themselves for an illusionary hope and, in masochistic self-torture, they endure something that a decisive change could long since have put in order.

Hopeful martyrs never realize that they are fleeing the real problem, for they believe they are constantly brooding over that very problem. In reality, they flee into their brooding because they refuse to give up their illusions or recognize reality.

The expectant visionary (p. 116)   **D4**

In inner conflict with his or her armored knight
Self-flight and self-constraint

The armored knight (p. 119)   **4D**

In inner conflict with his or her expectant visionary
Self-constraint and self-flight

THE "TYPOLOGY" OF THE 4-COLOR PERSON

Naturally, there is no typology of the 4-Color Person, for a normal person with an inner equilibrium and without prejudices does not have fixed behavior patterns when dealing with other people.

If you are fortunate enough to know someone whom you can't fit into the Color Disk because none of the twenty-four types is characteristic of him or her, then you are dealing with a 4-Color Person. One whose:

- senses of self are normal, not over- and not under-valued.
- self-respect makes him or her a nobleman.
- self-confidence makes him or her a Robinson Crusoe.
- self-moderation makes him or her a Diogenes.
- self-development makes him or her a Hans-in-Luck.

These four normal types are in such people and combine into the six normal senses of self:

- Self-respect and self-development make them self-reliant.
- Self-respect and self-confidence make them self-assured.
- Self-respect and self-moderation make them earnest.
- Self-development and self-confidence make them cheerful.

- Self-development and self-moderation make them carefree.
- Self-moderation and self-confidence make them satisfied.

But you want to know their behavior, not only their senses of self, just as you can check out the behavior of the types on the Color Disk. There's only one thing to say to that: Their behavior matches the basic ethical norms which you know. I've assembled them here in an overall diagram. Inside, you'll find the senses of self, and outside, the ethical attitudes of the 4-Color Person.

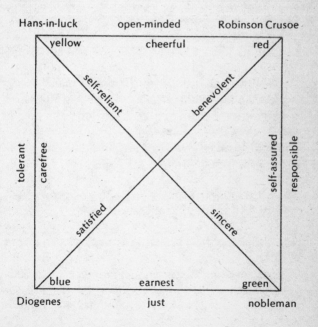

3
THE
COLORS

The Psychological
Effect of the Colors

I've told you very little as yet about the meaning of the
four primary colors. If you've got the time and interest
to find out about the colors as the mother tongue of the
unconscious, especially if you want to know and understand other people better, then it will be useful for
you to have an exact and comprehensive knowledge of
the colors.

As you know, one can form the four basic colors,
yellow, red, blue, and green, into a complete, harmonious color disk. The circle is the symbol of wholeness and harmony.

Those two ideals, wholeness and harmony, are
guidelines for 4-Color People. They strive for wholeness: on the one hand, by realizing themselves and
their potential in every area of the four primary colors;
on the other hand, by bringing these areas together
into a harmonious, well-balanced interrelationship.

As I have said, the sight of every color arouses a
certain emotion. You perceive that orange-red triggers
a totally different emotion in you than dark blue. You

feel something different with fir-green than with bright yellow.

When I was in school, people "knew" that different colors inspire different feelings. But "science" was of the opinion that every individual responds differently to a specific color, say orange-red.

This claim, "demonstrated by experiment," left me rather confused. I would have to live in an unintelligible chaos if I experienced orange-red as exciting, stimulating, activating, lively, while the same color had a soporific effect on someone else.

Could I truly understand another person if he or she saw the very same orange-red, the very same brightness or darkness, if that person encountered the very same tone, warmth, and movement, and yet perceived them and felt them as something different?

Well, "science" was in error. Today, after hundreds of thousands of Color Tests have been given in the United States, Europe, Africa, Japan, and Australia, we know that every specific color inspires not only the same perceptional stimulus, but also exactly the same experiential stimulus in every single individual, no matter what that person's culture may be. Orange-red has a stimulating effect on everyone, and dark blue has a relaxing effect on everyone. Therein lies the universal validity of color psychology.

The thing that is individual, however, is the personal liking, the indifference or antipathy that a person feels toward a color, for example, toward stimulating orange-red or relaxing dark blue. A person who desires stimuli and stimulation will find orange-red appealing. Someone who is overstimulated and exhausted won't endure orange-red. He or she finds it provoking and aggressive and rejects it. Thus every color has a certain objective universal experience quality. But—and herein lies its secret—that same color produces an emotional experience, an affect. Emotional experiences cannot be weighed, they cannot be measured by any yardstick, observed under any microscope, handled by any tweezers. Strong emotional experiences trigger bodily reactions. These bodily reactions can be measured. But the things we cannot measure are the emotional experiences themselves. Yet they are the crux when I am glad, filled with love, when I am enthusiastic, full of doubts, or full of hope.

Just as music inspires feelings, renders moods, and expresses the very subtlest emotions, so too the colors, through their hue, degree of lightness, and intensity, arouse the very same specific sensations in every individual.

Whether this sensation (like the exciting stimulus in orange) is appealing or unpleasant depends on a person's present emotional state—that is, the individual's sense of self. This subjective attitude toward the color is crucial in my Color Test's judgment of the individual personality. For us at the moment, however, only the objective, universal sensations in connection with the four primary colors are important.

The light colors, yellow and orange-red, have a discentric effect. The dark colors, dark blue and fir-green, have a concentric effect. That's why people say that light colors are active or warm, and dark colors passive or cold.

I avoid these terms. *Warm* and *cold* are tactile similes. They neither describe the optical color effect nor do they make a clear psychological statement. Similarly, the terms *active* and *passive* are unclear. *Passivity* can refer to both relaxation and rigidity.

Yellow, the lightest color, seems to dissolve into brightness. It is therefore subject to outside laws; it is heteronomous. Dark blue, on the other hand, seems to dissolve in darkness. It is also heteronomous.

Red and fir-green, in contrast, are in the middle with their medium lightness. They are fixed, solid, hence self-defining, autonomous.

These dry, abstract definitions should perhaps be fleshed out with life and experiences so that you can empathize with them. First, I want to bring you close to the contrasting pair red and blue, then green and yellow.

THE MEANING OF RED

You probably know the childhood rhyme:

> Red is love,
> And blood is red,
> Red is the devil
> In his fury red.

Love and fury seem like incompatible opposites. Yet they have something in common: Both are feelings of strong excitement. Love is an appealing excitement, fury an unappealing one. We speak of somebody as "seeing red" when that person is irritated and furious.

We can put the chaos of vulgar "color psychology" into order quickly if we make a fundamental distinction: Every feeling, whether excitement (red) or relaxation (blue), can always be seen from two viewpoints: pleasurable and appealing or unpleasurable and unappealing.

Red as pleasure is love, appetite, strength.

Red as displeasure is fury, disgust, overexcitement.

Blue as pleasure is relaxation, satisfaction, harmony.

Blue as displeasure is paralyzing tranquillity, deadly boredom; hence dissatisfaction, agitation, disquiet.

Colors arouse specific feelings. Since the color stimulus is transmitted from the eye, through the autonomic nervous system, into the interbrain, these feelings seem to arise in the interbrain. This part of the brain controls the nervous system and the pituitary gland. They, in turn, are responsible for the coordination of the organs. No wonder, then, that animals react to colors with the same physical processes.

An Algerian scientist, Benoît, covered the eyes of drakes with black blindfolds. Their sexual activity diminished. Then he put drakes under orange-red light for 120 hours. Their testicles almost doubled in size. Their sexual activity increased.

Since colors, independent of consciousness, affect the autonomic nervous system directly, the Color Test is a simple way of helping the physician to determine the patient's mental and physical state. All the doctor has to do is put the Color Test before the patient and ask, "Which color do you like and which color do you dislike?"

The effect of a specific color on the autonomic nervous system is the same in all people. Red affects all of them in a certain way and dark blue in a different way. If you look at one color for a while, your pulse and respiration will quicken, your blood pressure increase. With the other color, these three autonomic physical reactions are toned down. Think about what happens with red and what happens with dark blue.

When American students, as guinea pigs, stared at the orange-red of the Lüscher Color Test for a while, their autonomic physical functions increased. When the same students were shown the dark blue of the test, their nervous systems reacted in the opposite way. They relaxed. Their pulses calmed down, their blood pressure sank, and they breathed more slowly.

What happened to those students happens to all people throughout the world. The "language" of colors is international. It is not tied to any race or culture.

More than a decade ago, the research done by
W. Eggert in Berlin ("Diagnostik funktioneller Syndrome
mit dem Lüscher-Farbtest," *Materia Medica* No. 54,
Nordmark, 1965) confirmed the following: People
whose inner stress makes them prone to heart attack
prefer red and green in the color test (Red: activity;
blue-green: tension of willpower—inner tension). Then
come the colors reflecting the acute, autonomic state.
In the person in danger of having a heart attack, they
are gray and brown, the two colors of exhaustion. The
peril is even worse with a rejection of dark blue, which
means relaxation: "I can't afford to relax." Dim
lighting, which has an erotic effect, is naturally red.
And red lights anywhere in the world point the way to
where sexual excitement is sold.

Among the few painters who managed to verbalize
what color expresses was Vasily Kandinsky. In *Über
das Geistige in der Kunst* ("On the Spiritual in Art"),
he gave a precise description of red. He said that it has
an internal effect "as a very lively, bright, unquiet
color, which, however, does not have the frivolity of
yellow, which exhausts itself in all directions."

The painter Arnold Böcklin spent weeks trying to
produce a passionately glowing orange-red in order to
paint the cloth on which the bewitching Calypso sits.

In his well-known painting *The Three Red Horses*,
Franz Marc made the horses red because they have an
impulsive, excitable temperament. He used red for
what was really a brown skin because he wanted to
depict the mental expression.

In African love letters consisting of a chain of col-
ored beads, the red ones signify: "I love you
passionately. I have a great yearning for you."

Red is exciting. That's why it has an impact on the
viewer. That's why red is the color in the mantles of

kings and cardinals as it was in the hem of the senatorial toga.

Rimbaud, who wrote a poem about the meanings of the colors, felt that a woman who wears red can be easily seduced.

In religious symbolism, the color is used significantly. Red is the flame on the heads of those illuminated by the Pentecostal spirit.

Ernst Jünger, in *Lob der Vokale* ("In Praise of Vowels"), concludes: "Red is the color of domination and rebellion." He is thus acknowledging the arousing effect of the color.

Red is also the banner of the Russian Revolution. Indeed, red, by its very essense, is revolution: upheaval, energy in motion.

Red is energetic penetration and re-creation as soon as it is tinged yellow and becomes vermilion. The person who feels powerful, vital, energetic, thus having a sense of self corresponding to red, feels strong.

However, the person who is weak and encounters a strong person perceives the latter as threatening. That is why things that point to imminent dangers are painted red. The red traffic light forces the cars to halt in order to avoid the danger of a collision. Fire-fighting equipment and fire engines are red, because they are meant to express a "red alert." Here, the arousal of red becomes excitement.

Red as arousal, stimulation, as activity, fun, and creative willpower, is the symbolic color of a person who knows how to use his or her strength and ability. Red is the color of strength and self-confidence.

THE MEANING OF BLUE

WANDERER'S NIGHTSONG

Above all mountains
The sky is calm.
In all the treetops,
You barely sense
A breath of wind.
The birds fall silent in the woods.
Just wait, soon you
Will be resting too.

The famous writer of this famous poem, which renders the mood of blue so accurately, is Johann Wolfgang von Goethe. That same poet considered his scientific color theory more important than his poetry. He still has found few followers in that scientific field. On the other hand, he succeeded in verbalizing about certain colors, and his efforts are among the best descriptions of prescientific color psychology.

In Paragraph 781 of his *Farbenlehre* ("Theory of Colors"), Goethe says:

"We like to follow an object that flees from us, and, similarly, we like to look at blue, not because it presses in on us but because it pulls us after it."

With his extraordinary eloquence, he describes blue as an "attractive void."

Then again, Kandinsky is particularly expressive. "The tendency of blue to get deeper is so great that its deeper hues become more intense and seem more characteristic, more intimate. The deeper the blue, the more it summons man into infinity, arousing his yearning for purity and ultimately transcendence. Blue is the typical celestial color. Blue very profoundly develops the element of calm."

K. Köstlin, a little-known German author of the nineteenth century, writes about blue in his *Äesthetik* ("Aesthetics"; Tübingen, 1869): "Blue is an extremely tame and cooling contrast against anything disquieting, harsh, oppressive, or aggressive, an image of peace and gentleness, of refreshment; it is delicacy itself in the most revealing contrast against all material massiveness and heaviness." Kandinsky interprets blue as concentric motion.

Just sit down in front of a dark-blue color and see what kind of mood it produces in you. You will feel a motionless calm, a relaxed satisfaction; an endless sense of harmony and contentment will come over you.

If your wishes are fully satisfied, if what you have is enough for you in every way, then you will experience the complete pleasure, the contented serenity that comes from self-moderation. Self-moderation is the philosophy of life of Diogenes.

Which helps us to understand why Diogenes supposedly said to Alexander the Great, "If I weren't Diogenes, I would like to be Alexander the Great." If Diogenes hadn't found contentment in self-moderation (blue), then, like Alexander the Great, he would have had to strive continually for reassurance, strength, and imposing greatness (red) in a hectic intoxication for conquest (red). In blue, on the other hand, the color of self-moderation, contentment, and satisfaction, you feel relaxed and harmonious. You feel connected, attached, and secure. That is why blue corresponds to the attachment all around you: a sense of belonging. After all, we all know that "blue is the color of loyalty."

In a state of sensitive belonging, you are particularly alert to distinctions. Hence, blue corresponds to all kinds of sensitivity.

Blue, as relaxed sensitivity, is the prerequisite for empathy, aesthetic experience, and reflective meditation.

Schelling, in his *Philosophie der Kunst* ("Philosophy of Art"), uses nothing but blue symbols when he says: "Silence is the peculiar state of beauty, like the calm of undisturbed seas." Blue symbolically corresponds to the female, the horizontal direction, the left side, the phlegmatic temperament, the flourish in handwriting.

The German language has a word for the mood created by dark blue, a word that cannot be translated into other languages: *Gemüt*. Blue is the ideal of unity and harmony. It is primal maternal attachment, loyalty and trust, love and devotion (hence the blue cloak of Mary, Mother of God). Blue is symbolic of timeless eternity and of harmony in historical time, that is, tradition. Novalis, in his novel *Heinrich von Ofterdingen*, expressed romantic life in the symbol of the blue flower:

"He was overcome by a kind of sweet slumber, in which he dreamed of indescribable events. He found himself on soft grass at the edge of a spring. Dark-blue crags with gaudy veins loomed at a distance. The daylight surrounding him was brighter and milder than usually. The sky was blackish blue and utterly pure. The thing that drew him with full might was a tall, pale-blue flower, which stood right by the spring and touched him with its broad, shining petals. He saw nothing but the blue flower and he gazed and gazed at it with ineffable tenderness."

The German psychiatrist F. Stöffler wrote in "Hölderlins Äther und die Seelenharmonie" ("Hölderlin's Ether and Spiritual Harmony"; *Ärtzliche Praxis* No. 6, 1976):

"One quickly notes that Hölderlin, especially in his novel *Hyperion*, keeps using the adjective *blue* for the ether, thereby linking the blue of the sky to the notion of the ether. The repeated recurrence of blue encourages us to consult modern color psychology. Max Lüscher, the color psychologist, expressly describes blue as the color of harmony, of identification. The mention of harmony makes us perk up our ears when we recall that Hölderlin's work is filled with the leitmotiv of a striving for harmony between the self and the world. Noticeably, Hölderlin's blue either is mentioned and invoked with experiences in which man harmoniously identifies with his environment. In *Hyperion*, the young hero has such an intense experience with nature, which makes him one with the world: 'Lost in the distant blueness, I often glance up at the ether and into the holy sea, and I feel as if a kindred spirit is opening its arms to me, as if the pain of solitude is dissolving into the life of the deity. To be one with everything, that is the life of the deity, that is the heaven of man. To be one with everything that lives, to return to blissful self-oblivion, to the cosmos of nature, that is the peak of thoughts and joys, that is the holy mountain peak, the place of everlasting rest.' "

THE MEANING OF GREEN

If I ask you, "What does green mean?" you may promptly think of the phrase: "Green is hope." Now green can in fact signify hope, but only in the special hue of young leaves and buds in the spring. Only yellow-green, as an expectant opening of the self, corresponds to hope.

In total contrast to yellow-green, we have blue-green. And in contrast to blue-green, we have brown-green, which arouses the opposite feelings and sensations.

When I speak of green as a symbolic color, I expressly and exclusively mean fir-green, which is more of a dark and somewhat bluish hue.

The striking, highly stimulating motion of yellow, and the opposite, the relaxing and retiring motion of blue, are maintained and preserved in green. That is why green is static. Green has no externally operating kinetic energy, only a pent-up potential energy. This dammed energy, however, does not rest in the true sense of the word. It operates within itself as an internal tension structure and is static on the outside.

To be sure, Kandinsky writes: "Passivity is the striking feature of absolute green." However, he is obviously confusing static and passive—as many other people do.

The more a darkening blue is added to the green, the more solid, the colder, the tenser, harder, and more resistant the psychological effect of the color.

Just as molecules form a tension structure in a solid body, a structure that cannot be seen from the outside, so too, in every person, the self-referring, autonomous, concentric feelings from a tension structure. It is people's attitude toward themselves, which they experience as "self" or "ego" in the narrower sense.

Fir-green produces that very emotional state that we have defined as concentric, as a self-determining, autonomous attitude. Every morning when I get up, I establish that I am I, with all my memories and plans, of which I once again become aware.

But now let's put aside the logical dissecting knife and let's simply say: Fir-green corresponds to stability, solidity, constancy, persistence, resilience of the will; and, in regard to the sense of self, a feeling of self-worth. Fir-green corresponds to an authentic stable sense of self-worth, the self-respect of people who defy all inner or outer challenges and have the courage of their convictions.

Inflexible, solid fir-green corresponds to the nobleman's motto: *"Noblesse oblige."*

THE MEANING OF YELLOW

The fourth basic color is yellow. It is the lightest bright color. It is closest to white light.

In nature, the sun seldom appears in a yellow color. We see it as a dazzling light in the sky or as a radiant orange on the horizon. Nevertheless, the notion of yellow is involuntarily associated with the sun, and children paint the sun yellow. Everything the sun shines upon is bright and has a yellowish shimmer from the light reflex. Yellow seems like the sun: light and bright. Yellow seems easy, radiant, stimulating, and hence warming.

After white, yellow is the color that most strongly reflects the light hitting it. The light looks as if it were merely gliding across the bright surface.

Surface-ness is characteristic of yellow in many ways. The brightness of yellow and the polished, brilliant surface complement one another in the splendor of dazzling gold. Yellow as the color of surface appears not to hide any secret, and neither Goethe nor Kandinsky reveal more about the nature of yellow than what we immediately feel.

Goethe: "It is the color closest to light. In its utmost purity, it always implies the nature of brightness and has a cheerful, serene, gently stimulating character. Hence, experience teaches us that yellow makes a thoroughly warm and comforting impression. This warming effect can be noticed most keenly when one looks at a landscape through a yellow glass, especially on gray winter days. The eye is pleased, the heart cheered, the mind delighted, an immediate warmth seems to waft toward us."

Likewise, Kandinsky points out that "yellow tends so greatly toward lightness (white), that there can be no such thing as very dark yellow. If one looks at a circle filled with yellow, one notices that the yellow radiates, a motion comes from the center and approaches us almost visibly." Kandinsky experiences "the first motion of yellow, the striving toward the person, which can be intensified to a point of obtrusiveness (if the intensity of the yellow is increased), and also the second motion of the yellow, the leap across the border, the dispersal of energy in the environment . . . streaming out aimlessly on all sides."

Green is concentric tension and persistence. Yellow, in contrast, is discentric dissolution and alteration. If we liken green to pent-up, static, potential energy, then yellow would correspond to dynamic, kinetic energy.

Yellow is a basic color. It corresponds to the basic need of free development. Yellow is preferred by people looking for altered, liberating conditions, driven by wanderlust to go off on long voyages. Likewise, people who love flying, who like to leave the ground of reality, often prefer the color yellow.

Yellow as relaxation, as alteration, as liberation, as vast spaciousness, contrasts with green, which expresses tension, persistence, solidity, and narrow space.

Since yellow transmits a feeling of vastness, of change, of development, of liberation and ease, it is also regarded as the color of illumination and salvation. In these terms, the aureole of Christ the Savior is yellow. Likewise, Buddhist monks wear orange-yellow. Whatever color Hans-in-Luck may have worn, he is the cheerful, carefree yellow type.

THE PSYCHOLOGY AND PHILOSOPHY OF THE 4-COLOR PERSON

Structural Functional
Psychology

I'm delighted that your interest is still keen and that you now want to get into the intellectual background of the 4-Color Person. You have, it seems, learned how to deal with *functional psychology*. That is the basis of the Lüscher Color Test, which, for decades now, has been applied hundreds of thousands of times, all over the world, in clinical medicine, psychiatry, psychology, criminology, anthropology, personnel hiring, and education, in over ten languages.

Functional psychology is a simple system, which anyone can easily grasp and apply. And I'd like to explain its theory to you. I especially want to justify the fourness, which you already know as a 4-Color Person.

You like to ask why. Otherwise you'd have long since tossed *The 4-Color Person* on the shelf of books that you'll read someday when you have the time.

Well, why the fourness? Why do we think the way we have to think? Let's start at the beginning.

THE CATEGORIES OF STRUCTURE

Position

Think of something. It can be something pleasant. Well, if you can't think of anything better, then think of yourself.

Whether you like it or not, you have a position. You think of your professional, political, religious position, or your position in your family, club, in public or in bed. At any rate, you always have a position. And if you try to avoid it, where are you? In the position of a shirker. Thus, the designation of a position (posture, state, condition, arrangement, order) is the first necessary distinction we make when we want to judge something, for example: here, not there; yesterday, not today; a lot more, not so little; far more expensive, not so cheap; better than; more beautiful than.

The either/or began with Adam. When he took Eve as his wife, she brought him an anatomical dowry of the male/female difference. They found this so charming that they first applied it to all sorts of things, possible and then impossible things. And it has remained like that to the present day. The anatomical concepts soon become psychological or sociological misconceptions for glorifying or disqualifying the female sex.

C. G. Jung spoke about it much later, and more beautifully, in Latin: He taught that there is such a thing as an animus and an anima. Perhaps this was too Latin or too obvious. In any case, the concepts of animus for a "male" authoritarian behavior and anima for a "female" receptive position have never been popular.

So Eric Berne chose a more graphic image. He calls the "male" authoritarian, decisive behavior the "parental ego." And he calls the so-called "female" behavior, the receptive or easily influenced position, the "childhood ego."

One can cry, as Goethe did: "Two souls, alas, are dwelling in my breast!" Or one can divide the world, as the ancient Chinese did, into Yin and Yang. Or one can speak of X and Y. Whatever pair of words one uses, the important thing is that generally popular concepts, like male/female, are usually only symbols for two opposite positions.

Since such images mislead one into taking them too literally as a reality, I would rather say the same thing in Greek. I distinguish two positions: *autonomous* and *heteronomous*.

These words of Greek origin have the advantage of describing what is meant. And above all, they do not disqualify the female sex (like using "female" to connote weak, inferior, vague, soft).

We therefore distinguish two positions:

Autonomous: The subject determines, influences the object or partner (authoritarian or dominating).

Heteronomous: The subject is determined, influenced by the object or the partner (receptive, credulous, or enthusiastic).

However, when Adam, a male, credulously let himself be talked into eating the apple instead of demand-

ing a hot meal, he was behaving like a "female," that
is to say, heteronomously. He let himself be
influenced, and that was very "unmanly." Actually,
however, since Adam and Eve, every human being,
male or female, has behaved either autonomously or
heteronomously, depending on the situation and on
their taste.

You can differentiate people according to various
aspects, no matter what their name, whether they are
fat or thin, whether you like them or not.

But if you want to get down to the nitty-gritty,
because you have to work or live with someone, then
it's better to determine whether that person tends to
take an autonomous, influencing position, whether he
or she is tone-setting, initiating, self-sufficient, or even
authoritarian or self-willed, or whether that person
adjusts heteronomously and lets himself or herself be
influenced or controlled. Heteronomous people easily
get enthusiastic, they are sensitive and subject to
strong emotional influences: sheer joy or utter despair.
They are usually open-minded and sympathetic, often
fond of artistic, aesthetic impressions.

In regard to the Lüscher Color Test, let me quote the
heteronomous attitude, which has been verified hundreds of thousands of times (when blue and yellow are
preferred): "Strives for a happy, satisfying love relationship. Is capable of strong emotional enthusiasm.
Is helpful and adjusts compliantly in order to achieve
the loving togetherness he aspires to. Requires rapport
and understanding."

From the same test, let me also quote the opposite,
autonomous position (when green and red are preferred): "Wants to get his way and overcome obstacles
and hindrances. Wants to make up his own mind and
follows his goal with consistency and initiative. Refuses to depend on the good will of others."

Direction

The second required distinction is direction. For instance, you can focus on something special, and always only on that. You can concentrate all your interests on a certain point, like a bull's-eye. You can think mainly about yourself, your inner world, or else your mate, or a certain constant goal in the outer world. I call this concentric direction toward a certain steady goal *stable*. Thus, the ego is extremely concentric. For instance, you know that you are always the same every morning when you wake up.

In a drawing, it looks like this:

However, when the direction goes from you or from a point to many sides and changing objects, then we call this *mobile*. The mobile, extravert direction leads to the people around you, to changing situations and contacts.

In a drawing, it looks like this:

C. G. Jung similarly distinguished two directions, namely *introversion* and *extroversion*.

Using the Color Test (red and yellow), let me show you how this mobile behavior manifests itself:

"Striving for experience and success. Wants to develop freely without being inhibited by self-doubts. Wants to win out and have intense experiences. Likes to be with people, prone to enthusiasm, is open to new and modern things. Has many interests and wants to widen his field of activity. Is full of expectations and looks forward to the future."

Intensive behavior is described in the Color Test as follows: "Needs calm, peaceful harmony. Would like to ease tensions peacefully, without hostile confrontations. Tries to master situations and tasks in a gingerly fashion. Is extremely tactful, sensitive, and observant of fine details."

Now, a person acts autonomously or heteronomously according to the situation. And likewise, you change your direction. Lying in bed, you can focus on yourself, think about someone dear to you, or mull over your favorite subject. Your thoughts take a stable course. In city traffic, however, a man can save his skin only with extravert attention. If he stares intensively at some woman's breasts, his car can easily wind up as an extravert pile of scrap.

The Four Basic Structures

I've loaded you with all kinds of things to think about. If you've shared all the effort with me, then you'll draw your profit. You see, we've made the components of a computer, and all we have to do now is fit them together. You can use the computer whenever you feel like understanding the complexities of a situation or person. The computer's parts consist of two positions (autonomous and heteronomous) and two directions (stable and mobile).

THE FOUR FIELDS OF THE FOUR COLORS		POSITION	
		HETERONOMOUS	AUTONOMOUS
DIRECTION	mobile (changing objects)	YELLOW a) experiencing new things b) looseness c) change d) potential e) vastness f) form for yellow	RED a) influencing others b) excitement c) activity d) multiplicity e) wealth of stimuli f) form for red
	stable (same object)	BLUE a) experiencing self b) calm, relaxation c) satisfaction d) unity e) wealth of stimuli f) form for blue	GREEN a) determining self b) tensions c) persistence d) necessity e) narrowness f) form for green

Position and direction are in fact always combined. I call this combining *structure*. Two positions times two directions thus make four basic structures. Let me illustrate these basic structures as four fields with the four basic colors red, blue, green, and yellow.

Total opposites exist between the yellow field and the green field as well as between the red field and the blue field.

These four fields are basic structures *(archetypes)* of experience. They are four distinct mental qualities or states. We can designate them as neutral states with an equal sign: = .

The same is expressed by the four basic forms.

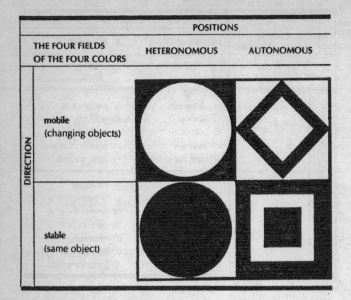

You and I and everyone else, we are all in one of these four states (or a mixture thereof): for example, calm and satisfied (blue) or aroused and active (red). We also experience every object in one of these four states (or a mixture thereof): for example, a calm landscape or a relaxed, free and easy friendship (blue), or stirring music or an angry argument (red).

THE CATEGORIES OF FUNCTION

If you come along on these next few steps and enjoy understanding complexities, then I'll be delighted. At the same time, let me thank you for becoming so interested and confident through our conversation that you're willing to discuss further ideas (only in an anonymous dialogue, alas) aside from any direct use for your 4-Color well-being.

The Four Dimensions

With the four basic structures, we have already gotten to know the first two dimensions of the system of functional psychology:

1. As the first dimension, as principles of order, the positions or attitudes, autonomous and heteronomous, were distinguished.
2. As the second dimension, the two directions, intensive and extensive, were distinguished.

These two dimensions form the four fields (archetypes) of the four basic colors, which I have called the four basic structures.

Now let's mention a few psychological terms, which you may know and which mean the same or a similar thing.

C. G. Jung's four functions may be assigned to our four basic structures. Even his term *extroverted* is almost identical with *extensive*. On the other hand, his term *introverted* is ambiguous. It contains parts of both the intensive direction and the defense tactic. You see, *introversion* also refers to the defense stance against disturbing situations (brooding, self-control, self-pity, depressing disappointment). His distinction between *animus* and *anima* can be assigned to our polarity of *autonomous/heteronomous*. Eric Berne, who became popular with his **parental ego/childhood ego** distinction, is describing the polarity between autonomous and heteronomous. Since this simple polarity is indeed simplistic, he was forced to subdivide the parental and the childhood ego into a concentric and a discentric attitude—four types. What he means by the *parental ego* is nothing else than our 4-Color Person. One-dimensional systems like introversion/extroversion or parental ego/childhood ego are inadequate.

On the other hand, two-dimensional systems were already used by the ancient Babylonians in their astrological typology. Heraclitus (500 B.C.) and—quite expressly—the philosopher Empedocles (395–434 B.C.) distinguish the four elements: fire (red), water (blue), earth (green), and air (yellow). Empedocles also believed there are "basic colors equal in number to the elements" (four basic colors). More popular, even today, is the theory of temperaments advanced by the Roman physician Hippocrates (400 B.C.). He distinguishes the

- choleric (red type)
- phlegmatic (blue type)
- melancholic (green type)
- sanguine (yellow type).

After two and a half millennia, it is time we opted for three- and four-dimensional systems instead of reverting to one-dimensional ones.

3. Thus, for the third dimension, we designate: motion.
4. And for the fourth dimension, we recognize the change in motion.

We will now go into the details of the third and fourth dimensions.

Motion

The third dimension comes about through the change in a state, in motion, and in these two directions:

Acceptance, goal tactic (+): positiveness, sympathy;

Rejection, defense tactic (−): negativeness, antipathy.

For instance, if I'm in an autonomous/concentric green state, I can change in multiple directions: I can open up to additional information and new possibilities (yellow) or I can try to get my own way in an offensive battle (red). The change toward a desirable state we call acceptance or goal tactic and we designate it with $\gg + \ll$.

If, on the other hand, my subjective state does not harmonize with my objective situation, then I'll use some tactic to protect myself against that situation. With this defense tactic, I try to get away from the undesirable situation. The change of a state by rejection, a defense tactic, and turning against it will be marked with $\gg - \ll$.

Of course, there is always the third possibility that my subjective state is congruent with the objective situation. That is the case when I am content and happy. There is no changing movement, and that is indicated with the sign of inner equilibrium, $\gg = \ll$.

Change in Movement

The forth dimension comes about by changing movement, and it is very important in conflict psychology (neuroses):

a. The motion tempo changes through acceleration, in a driven addiction, say, for alcohol, nicotine, or drugs. This driven state is known to everyone at least as a torturous yearning or a sudden fear, as when, for instance, an expected partner stands you up without even calling.

b. The motion tempo changes through deceleration, stagnation, and fixation on certain needs (obsessions, phobias, defense attitudes) and modifications (inhibited needs, perversions, suppression of affection and sex, aggression or assertion).

The accelerated emotions and the fixated emotions are known as "neurotic" behavior. In the Lüscher Full Color Test, the neurotic accelerations appear as a unilaterally exaggerated preference for a color tendency: full columns ("I absolutely have to have . . ."). Neurotic decelerations appear as a unilaterally excessive rejection of a color tendency: empty columns ("I simply can't stand . . .").

Functional Psychology

In the four fields of the four colors I have
under (a)   the definition of functional psychology
under (b)   the psycho-autonomic state
under (c)   the psychological behavior
under (d)   the logical term
under (e)   the corresponding spatial meaning
under (f)   the archetypal forms derived from form psychology and, when statistically documented, corresponding to the four basic colors of the Color Test.

The logical categories under (d) fully overlap with those of Kant.

KANT'S CATEGORIES AND THOSE OF STRUCTURAL FUNCTIONAL PSYCHOLOGY

The great German philosopher Immanuel Kant examined our thought processes. In his category table, he assembled the necessary thinking tools, the thought categories with which we judge something.

Thus, he distinguishes possibility and necessity. That corresponds to yellow and green precisely. He also distinguishes unity and plurality. That is exactly what we mean by blue and red.

He also cites causality. That is the relationship of the foregoing cause and the following effect. Causality exists between the foregoing possibility (yellow) and the chronologically following necessity (green) of the effect that has occurred. According to Kant, this relationship, "time," is the one "form of contemplation" of everything we experience.

Furthermore, he lists interaction (or community) as a thought category. In the very same way, there is an interaction or community relationship between unity (blue) and plurality (red). In the Color Test, the favoring of red and blue is described as follows: "Strives for a harmonious life and closeness. Regular activity and a loving relationship, especially within the family, are prerequisites for happiness. Tries to achieve a trusting and emotional relationship with the people close to him."

Interaction between multiple objects forms a community or unity. Space forms the unity for the plurality of objects. According to Kant, space is the second form of contemplation of everything we experience.

Space and time, Kant's two forms of contemplation, are thus the coordinates in the system of functional psychology. They are the axes from blue (unity) to red (plurality) and from yellow (possibility) to green (necessity).

THE EXACTNESS OF PSYCHOLOGICAL NORMS

All this may sound dry and matter-of-fact to you. However, psychological insights can be gained only through observations and terminologically exact analyses. Statistical figures say something only when interpreted according to their psychological meaning. Numbers can never be more than quantitative, sociological data on, say, how often certain behavior occurs in a group of people. But no number can ever provide a psychological explanation for any behavior. That's why we need psychological norms, which are defined as categories of a notional system.

Anyone who has learned how to think critically demands that statements be proved with irrefutable logic. No such person will thoughtlessly accept ideal norms—whether from a religious, a political, or a scientific ideology.

With the help of functional psychology (mathematical function: the dependence of a quantity from a specific other quantity), the psychological norms can be determined precisely and logically and proved scientifically.

Functional psychology is the system of a four-dimensional whole. Its exactness lies in the irrefutable definition of the necessary relations within the psychological whole (I, autonomous-heteronomous; II, intensive-extensive; III, acceptance-rejection; IV, acceleration-deceleration). Functional psychology is a system of relations that is mathematical, hence precisely defined and logically irrefutable.

It is also an exact science if its defined, systemic relations are always verifiably consistent with reality. Mathematics can be applied to astronomy or to the periodic system of chemistry. And likewise, with the help of the system of functional psychology, we can theoretically derive psychological behavior forms in advance, before they are even observed in individual cases. The subsequent statistical and empirical confirmation, the research results of the functional psychology Color Test and the Form Test in psycho-somatic medicine, psychiatry, criminology, and anthropology, prove the scientific exactness of these foundations of functional psychology.

THE LOGIC OF AESTHETICS

A logical elucidation, as presented in the last few chapters, is something that I perceive as aesthetic harmony. Understanding the dynamics in the wealth of life's experiences is something I experience as happiness and pleasure, like Bach's *Brandenburg* concerti.

Functional psychology applies the categories of logical distinction (autonomous-heteronomous and intensive-extensive) to define the aesthetic effect of colors and forms. Functional psychology makes the common features and the kinship of logic and aesthetics obvious. I have used precisely these criteria in constructing both the Form Test and the Color Test. Hence both tests structurally match the logical, psycho-logical, and aesthetic differentiation criteria (see the four-field diagram of functional psychology, p. 000) that obtain in every individual and every culture. This has been empirically proved by hundreds of thousands of tests even outside of Europe and America.

Naturally, any aesthetic phenomena of forms, colors, and materials—like designs, packagings, architectural shapes, textiles—can be defined with these categories and described in terms of their psychological effects. For two decades now, this possibility has been successfully applied with great versatility in advertising and marketing.

THE LOGIC OF ETHICS

Philosophy has three areas: logic, ethics, and aesthetics. Not only has functional psychology's categories related logic and aesthetics more closely, but, more important than anything else, ethics has become a comprehensible and logically cogent moral doctrine for the first time.

We have defined, logically described and explained, the four ego norms (self-respect, self-confidence, self-moderation, self-development) with the logical categories (autonomous-heteronomous and intensive-extensive).

The logically proved four ego norms led, on the basis of the categorical imperative, to the six basic ethical norms: justice, open-mindedness, responsibility, tolerance, sincerity, benevolence (pp. 61–64).

LOGICAL ETHICS INSTEAD OF RELIGIOUS MORALITY

The basic ethical norms obtain for the 4-Color Person because they correspond to logically cogent insight. Four-Color People are mentally self-sufficient. That is why they won't have their morality—say, in the guise of the Ten Commandments—forced upon them.

They refuse to burden their lives with a faith that does not convince them with logical insight.

Religion had to yield one of its pillars, the explanation of nature, to science. This happened five hundred years ago, thereby ushering in the modern era.

Ever since, natural science and ethical theology have been adversaries. Science and faith are separated by a gap. The lack of an intellectual, spiritual tie has led technology on the one side and morality on the other side to a dead end. That is one of the causes of the crisis in our present-day culture.

Scientific technology has been overemphasized and left without moral guidance. Humanity has entered the path of self-destruction. People are using information and computer technology to pierce into man's private sphere in order to manipulate him. Since man is brainwashed by a dubious advertising psychology (likewise without moral guidance) and by the whole power of TV, radio, and newspapers into consuming certain political, social, and scientific "ideals," the Sunday morality of religion has lost its influence on daily life.

For the medieval artisan, high quality was the ideal. Today, quantity and turnover have become the ideals of success. Marketing exploits the neurotic mass needs (the yellow press, sexual animation, advertising for prestige consumption, for fashions, cosmetics, cars, alcohol, tobacco products) in order to pursue their morally inferior ideal of quantity.

For these reasons and because of free sexual mores, this pillar of religion is also crumbling.

However, the main reason why ethics based on religion have become ineffective and partially unbelievable is that their formulations and contents no longer suffice for modern psychological and sociological understanding (for example, the devil incarnate of the Catholic Church).

For the 4-Color Person, a new modern age has begun. Devout subservience, intellectual dependency, and undiscerning obedience are not his or her cup of tea.

Four-Color People intellectually stand on their own feet. They think independently. They act on their own honest conviction, according to a logically founded ethics.

The 4-Color Person is the person of the new modern age.

INDEX